THE PERSECUTION AND ASSASSINATION
OF MARAT AS PERFORMED BY
THE INMATES OF THE ASYLUM OF CHARENTON
UNDER THE DIRECTION OF THE MARQUIS DE SADE

PETER WEISS

The Persecution and Assassination of Marat as Performed by the Inmates of the Asylum of Charenton under the Direction of the Marquis de Sade

English version by Geoffrey Skelton
Verse adaptation by Adrian Mitchell

CALDER AND BOYARS LIMITED · LONDON

FIRST PUBLISHED IN GREAT BRITAIN IN 1965
BY JOHN CALDER (PUBLISHERS) LTD.

SECOND EDITION 1966
BY CALDER & BOYARS LTD.
18 BREWER STREET, LONDON, W.1.

THIRD EDITION 1967

FOURTH EDITION 1969

ORIGINALLY PUBLISHED IN GERMANY BY SUHRKAMP VERLAG,
1964
UNDER THE TITLE:

DIE VERFOLGUNG UND ERMORDUNG JEAN PAUL
MARATS DARGESTELLT DURCH DIE SCHAUSPIEL-
GRUPPE DES HOSPIZES ZU CHARENTON UNTER
ANLEITUNG DES HERRN DE SADE

All inquiries concerning the British and Commonwealth rights for professional or amateur stage production should be directed to The International Copyright Bureau Ltd., 26 Charing Cross Road, London, W.C.2.

All inquiries concerning Canadian rights for professional or amateur stage production should be directed to The Dramatic Publishing Co., 86 East Randolph St., Chicago, Illinois, 60601.

REPRODUCED AND PRINTED IN ENGLAND BY
LATIMER TREND & CO. LTD., WHITSTABLE

INTRODUCTION

What's the difference between a poor play and a good one? I think there's a very simple way of comparing them. A play in performance is a series of impressions; little dabs, one after another, fragments of information or feeling in a sequence which stir the audience's perceptions. A good play sends many such messages, often several at a time, often crowding, jostling, overlapping one another. The intelligence, the feelings, the memory, the imagination are all stirred. In a poor play, the impressions are well spaced out, they lope along in single file and in the gaps, the heart can sleep while the mind wanders to the day's annoyances and thoughts of dinner.

The whole problem of the theatre today is just this: how can we make plays dense in experience? Great philosophical novels are often far longer than thrillers, more content occupies more pages, but great plays and poor plays fill up evenings of pretty comparable length. Shakespeare seems better in performance than anyone else because he gives us more, moment for moment, for our money. This is due to his genius, but also to his technique. The possibilities of free verse on an open stage enabled him to cut the inessential detail and the irrelevant realistic action: in their place he could cram sounds and ideas, thoughts and images which make each instant into a stunning mobile.

Today we are searching for a twentieth-century technique that could give us the same freedom. For strange reasons, verse alone no longer does the trick: yet there is a device, Brecht invented it, a new device of quite incredible power. This what has been uncouthly labelled 'alienation'. Alienation is the art of placing an action at a distance so that it can be judged objectively and so that it can be seen in relation to the world—or rather, worlds—around it. Peter Weiss's play is a great tribute to alienation and breaks important new ground. Brecht's use of 'distance' has long been considered in opposition to Artaud's conception of theatre as immediate and violent subjective experience. I have never believed this to be true. I believe that theatre, like life, is made up of the unbroken conflict between impressions and judgments—illusion and disillusion cohabit painfully and are inseparable. This is just what Weiss achieves. Starting with its title, everything about this play is designed to crack the spectator on the jaw, then douse him with ice-cold water, then force him to assess intelligently what has happened to him, then give him a kick in the balls, then bring him back to his senses again. It's not exactly Brecht and it's not Shakespeare either but it's very Elizabethan and very much of our time.

Weiss not only uses total theatre, that time-honoured notion of getting all the elements of the stage to serve the play. His force is not only in the quantity of instruments he uses; it is above all in the jangle produced by the clash of styles. Everything is put in its place by its neighbour—the serious by the comic, the noble by the popular, the literary by the crude, the intellectual by the physical: the abstraction is vivified by the stage image, the violence illuminated by the cool flow of thought. The strands of meaning of the play pass to and fro through its structure and the result is a very complex form: like in Genet it is a hall of mirrors or a corridor of echoes—and one must keep looking front and back all the time to reach the author's sense.

One of the London critics attacked the play on the ground that it was a fashionable mixture of all the best theatrical ingredients around—Brechtian—didactic—absurdist—Theatre of Cruelty. He said this to disparage but I repeat this as praise. Weiss saw the use of every one of these idioms and he saw that he needed them all. His assimilation was complete. An undigested set of influences leads to a blur: Weiss's play is strong, its central conception startlingly original, its silhouette sharp and unmistakeable. From our practical experience I can report that the force of the performance is directly related to the imaginative richness of the material: the imaginative richness is the consequence of the amount of levels that are working simultaneously: this simultaneity is the direct result of Weiss's daring combination of so many contradictory techniques.

Is the play political? Weiss says it is Marxist and this has been much discussed. Certainly it is not polemical in the sense that it does not prove a case nor draw a moral. Certainly, its prismatic structure is such that the last line is not the place to search for the summing-up idea. The idea of the play is the play itself, and this cannot be resolved in a simple slogan. It is firmly on the side of revolutionary change. But it is painfully aware of all the elements in a violent human situation and it presents these to the audience in the form of a painful question.

'The important thing is to pull yourself up by your own hair
To turn yourself inside out and see the whole world with fresh eyes.'
—Marat

How? someone is bound to ask. Weiss wisely refuses to tell, he forces us to relate opposites and face contradictions. He leaves us raw. He searches for meaning instead of defining one and puts the responsibility of finding the answers back where it properly belongs. Off the dramatist and on to ourselves.

LONDON   PETER BROOK
1964

Royal Shakespeare Company in

The Persecution and Assassination of Marat as Performed by the Inmates of the Asylum of Charenton under the Direction of the Marquis de Sade

By Peter Weiss
English version by Geoffrey Skelton
Verse adaptation by Adrian Mitchell

M. Coulmier	Clifford Rose	
Mme. Coulmier	Brenda Kempner	
Mlle. Coulmier	June Baker	
Herald	Ian Richardson	
Kokol	Michael Williams	
Polpoch	Jonathan Burn	
Cucurucu	Freddie Jones	
Rossignol	Elizabeth Spriggs	
Jacques Roux	Robert Lloyd	
Charlotte Corday	Glenda Jackson	
Jean Paul Marat	Clive Revill	
Simonne Everard	Susan Williamson	
Marquis de Sade	Patrick Magee	
Duperret	John Steiner	
Abbot	Wyn Jones	
A mad animal	Morgan Sheppard	
Schoolmaster	Timothy West	
Mother	Wyn Jones	
Father	Henry Woolf	
A newly-rich lady	Geoffrey Hinsliff	
Voltaire	John Harwood	
Lavoissier	Leon Lissek	
Patients	Mary Allen	Mark Jones
	Jennifer Clulow	Caroline Maud
	Maroussia Frank	Lyn Pinkney
	June Jago	Bryan Stanyon
	Michael Jenkinson	
Nuns	Diana Bishop	Tamara Fuerst
Guards	Edward Clayton	Richard Williams

Musicians

Patrick Gowers	*Music Director/Harmonium*
Richard Callinan	*Percussion*
Michael Gould	*Trumpet*
Nicholas Moes	*Guitar/Harmonium*
Rainer Schulein	*Flute/Piccolo/Alto Flute*

Directed by	Peter Brook
Setting and properties designed by	Sally Jacobs
Associate designer	Elizabeth Duffield
Costumes designed by	Gunilla Palmstierna-Weiss
Lighting by	David Read
Assistant to the director	Malcolm Goddard
Music by	Richard Peaselee

First performance at the Aldwych Theatre 20th August 1964

THE PERSECUTION AND ASSASSINATION OF MARAT AS PERFORMED BY THE INMATES OF THE ASYLUM OF CHARENTON UNDER THE DIRECTION OF THE MARQUIS DE SADE

Drama in two acts by PETER WEISS

CHARACTERS

MARQUIS DE SADE	*sixty-eight years old, extremely corpulent, gray hair, smooth complexion. He moves heavily, breathes at times with difficulty, as if asthmatic. His clothing is of good quality, but worn. He is wearing white breeches with bows, a wide-sleeved white shirt with ornamental front and lace cuffs and white buckled shoes.*
JEAN-PAUL MARAT	*in his fiftieth year, suffering from a skin disease. He is draped in a white cloth and has a white bandage round his temples.*
SIMONNE EVRARD	*Marat's mistress, of indeterminate age. The player of the role is wearing a hospital uniform, with an apron and a headcloth. Her posture is crooked, her movements odd and constrained. When she has nothing to do, she stands wringing a cloth in her hands. She seizes every opportunity to change Marat's bandage.*
CHARLOTTE CORDAY	*aged twenty-four. Her clothing consists of a*

9

thin white blouse of Empire cut. The blouse does not conceal the bosom, but she wears a flimsy white cloth over it.

Her long auburn hair hangs down on the right side of her neck. She wears pink leather boots with high heels, and when she is 'on stage' a ribboned hat is tied to her.

She is attended throughout by two sisters, who support her, comb her hair and arrange her clothes. She moves like a somnambulist.

DUPERRET   *Girondist Deputy.*

The player of the role wears in addition to his hospital shirt a short waistcoat and the smooth tight trousers of an 'Incroyable'. His clothing is also white, with some ornamentation. He is held in the mental home as an erotomaniac, and takes advantage of his role as Corday's lover at every suitable opportunity.

JACQUES ROUX   *former priest, radical Socialist.*

He wears a white hospital shirt with an overall shaped like a monk's robe. The sleeves of his shirt are tied together in front of him over his hands, and he can move only in the limits of this strait-jacket.

THE FOUR SINGERS   *Part crowd types, part comedians. They have*
KOKOL, *Bass*   *decked out their hospital uniforms with gro-*
POLPOCH, *Baritone*   *tesque bits of costume and wear the cap of the*
CUCURUCU, *Tenor*   *revolution. Rossignol, with her tricolour sash*
ROSSIGNOL, *Soprano*   *and sabre represents the figure of Marianne.*
They have singing voices and perform in mime.

PATIENTS   *as extras, voices, mimes and chorus. According to need they appear either in their white hospital uniforms or in primitive costumes with strong colour contrasts. Any not required*

10

	in the play devote themselves to physical exercises. Their presence must set the atmosphere behind the acting area. They make habitual movements, turn in circles, hop, mutter to themselves, wail, scream and so on.
HERALD	*wears a harlequin smock over his hospital shirt. His two-pointed cap is hung with bells and spangles. He is draped with numerous instruments with which he can make a noise as necessary.*
	He holds in his hand a beribboned staff.
FIVE MUSICIANS	*Inmates of the mental home, clad in white. They play harmonium, lute, flute, trumpet and drums.*
MALE NURSES	*in light grey uniforms with long white aprons which give them the appearance of butchers. They carry batons in the pockets of their aprons.*
SISTERS	*also dressed in light grey with long white aprons, starched collars and large white bonnets. They carry rosaries. The sisters are played by athletic-looking men.*
COULMIER	*Director of the mental home, in elegant light grey clothing, with coat and top hat. He wears pince-nez and carries a walking stick. He likes to adopt a Napoleonic pose.*
COULMIER'S WIFE AND DAUGHTER	*form a composite pattern of colour from pale mauve to pearl grey, sprinkled with jewels and glittering silver.*

ACT ONE

The asylum bell rings behind the stage. The curtain rises.

1. ASSEMBLY

The stage shows the bath hall of the asylum. To right and left bathtubs and showers. Against the back wall a many-tiered platform with benches and massage tables. In the middle area of the stage benches are placed for the actors, sisters and male nurses. The walls are covered with white tiles to a height of about ten feet. There are window openings high up in the side walls. There is a metal framework in front of the platform and around the baths at the sides. Curtains are fixed to each side of the framework before the platform and these can be pulled when the patients are to be hidden. Front stage centre there is a circular acting arena. To the right of it a dais for MARAT's *bath, to the left a dais for* SADE's *chair. Left front a raised tribunal for* COULMIER *and his* FAMILY. *On another tribunal right front the musicians stand ready.*

SADE *is occupied with last-minute preparations for the entry of the actors.*

The MALE NURSES *are completing a few routine operations of bathing and massage. Patients are sitting or lying on the platform at the back.*

SADE *gives a sign. Through a side door right back the actors enter, led by* COULMIER *and his family and escorted by* SISTERS *and* MALE NURSES.

The PATIENTS *rise to their feet.*

The ceremonious procession comes forward. The asylum bell is still tolling.

MARAT, wrapped in a white sheet and accompanied by SIMONNE, is led to the bath.

CORDAY, sunk into herself, is taken to a bench by two sisters.

DUPERRET, ROUX and the FOUR SINGERS take up their positions as COULMIER reaches the stage. The HERALD stands in the middle of the stage. SADE stands near his raised chair. The tolling of the bell ceases.

The procession moves towards the acting area.

COULMIER enters the acting area.

The PATIENTS in the background stand tensely. One of them adopts an eccentric pose, another comes slowly forward with outstretched arms.

FANFARE.

2. PROLOGUE

COULMIER: As Director of the Clinic of Charenton
             I would like to welcome you to this salon
             To one of our residents a vote
             of thanks is due Monsieur de Sade who wrote
             and has produced this play for your delectation
             and for our patients' rehabilitation
             We ask your kindly indulgence for
             a cast never on stage before
             coming to Charenton But each inmate
             I can assure you will try to pull his weight
             We're modern enlightened and we don't agree
             with locking up patients We prefer therapy
             through education and especially art
             so that our hospital may play its part
             faithfully following according to our lights
             the Declaration of Human Rights
             I agree with our author Monsieur de Sade

that his play set in our modern bath house
won't be marred
by all these instruments for mental and physical
hygiene
Quite on the contrary they set the scene
For in Monsieur de Sade's play he has tried
to show how Jean-Paul Marat died
and how he waited in his bath before
Charlotte Corday came knocking at his door

3. PREPARATION

HERALD *knocks three times with his staff and gives the orchestra a*
sign.
Ceremonious music begins.
COULMIER *moves to his* FAMILY.
SADE *mounts his dais.*
MARAT *is placed in his bath.* SIMONNE *puts his bandage straight.*
The SISTERS *arrange* CORDAY'*s costume.*
The GROUP *assumes the pose of a heroic tableau.*

4. PRESENTATION

The music stops.
                    [*Herald knocks three times with his staff*]
HERALD: Already seated in his place
               here is Marat observe his face
               [*points his staff at* MARAT]
               Fifty years old and not yet dead
               he wears a bandage around his head
               [*points staff at bandage*]
               His flesh burns it is yellow as cheese
               [*points at his neck*]
               because disfigured by a skin disease
               And only water cooling every limb
               [*points to bath*]

prevents his fever from consuming him
  [MARAT *takes his pen and begins to write*]
To act this most important role we chose
a lucky paranoic one of those
who've made unprecedented strides since we
introduced them to hydrotherapy
The lady who is acting as his nurse
    [*points at* SIMONNE. *She bends with a jerky*
    movement over MARAT, *loosens his bandage and*
    puts on a new one]
whose touch certainly makes him no worse
is Simonne Evrard not Charlotte Corday
Marat and Evrard united one day
They shared one vision of the just and true
and furthermore they shared her money too
Here's Charlotte Corday waiting for her entry
    [*points to* CORDAY *who smoothes her clothes and*
    ties her neckcloth]
She comes from Caen her family landed gentry
Her dress is pretty shoes chic and you'll note
she readjusts the cloth around her throat
    [*points at it.* CORDAY *adjusts it*]
Historians agree so it's not lewd in us
to say that she's phenomenally pulchritudinous
    [*She draws herself up*]
Unfortunately the girl who plays the role here
has sleeping sickness also melancholia
Our hope must be for this afflicted soul
    [*With closed eyes, she inclines her head far*
    backwards]
that she does not forget her role
[*with emphasis, turning to* CORDAY]
Ah here comes Monsieur Duperret
[*indicates* DUPERRET]
with silken hose and fresh toupee

To the Revolution's murderous insanity
he brings a touch of high urbanity
Though as a well-known Girondist
his name's upon Marat's black list
he's handsome cheerful full of zest
and needs more watching than the rest
> [DUPERRET *approaches* CORDAY, *pawing her
> furtively. The* HERALD *raps him on the hand
> with his staff. A* SISTER *pulls back*
> DUPERRET.]

Jailed for taking a radical view
of anything you can name the former priest
   Jacques Roux
> [*indicates* ROUX *who pushes out his elbows and
> raises his head*]

Ally of Marat's revolution but
unfortunately the censor's cut
most of his rabble-rousing theme
Our moral guardians found it too extreme

ROUX: Liberty
> [*opens his mouth and pushes his elbows out
> vigorously.*
> COULMIER *raises his forefinger threateningly.*]

HERALD: Ladies and gentlemen our players
are drawn from many social layers
> [*He waves his staff over the audience and the
> group of actors*]

Our singers for example of these four
each must be classified as bottom drawer
But now they've left the alcoholic mists
of slums and gin cellars our vocalists
> [*points to the* FOUR SINGERS]

Cucurucu Polpoch Kokol
and on the streets no longer Rossignol

[*Each named changes his pose with a studied bow,* ROSSIGNOL *curtsies.*]
Now meet this gentleman from high society
[*points at* SADE *who turns his back on the public in a bored way*]
who under the lurid star of notoriety
came to live with us just five years ago
It's to his genius that we owe this show
The former Marquis Monsieur de Sade
whose books were banned his essays barred
while he's been persecuted and reviled
thrown into jail and for some years exiled
The introduction's over now the play
of Jean-Paul Marat can get under way
Tonight the date
is the thirteenth of July eighteen-o-eight
And on this night our cast intend
showing how fifteen years ago night without end
fell on that man that invalid
[*points at* MARAT]
And you are going to see him bleed
[*points at* MARAT'*s breast*]
and see this woman after careful thought
[*points at* CORDAY]
take up the dagger and cut him short
Homage to Marat
[*Music starts.* CORDAY *is led by the* SISTERS *from the arena to a bench in the background.* SIMONNE *seats herself on the edge of the dais behind* MARAT'*s bath.* SADE *goes to his seat and sits down.* ROUX *and* DUPERRET *withdraw to a bench.*]
[*The* FOUR SINGERS *take their position for the homage to* MARAT]

5. HOMAGE TO MARAT

KOKOL & [*Recitative*]
POLPOCH: Four years after the Revolution
and the old king's execution
four years after remember how
those courtiers took their final bow

CHORUS: [*singing in the background*]
String up every aristocrat
Out with the priests and let them live on their
fat

CUCURUCU & [*Recitative*]
ROSSIGNOL: Four years after we started fighting
Marat keeps on with his writing
Four years after the Bastille fell
he still recalls the old battle yell

CHORUS: [*singing in the background*]
Down with all of the ruling class
Throw all the generals out on their arse

ROUX: Long live the Revolution
[*The* FOUR SINGERS *and other* PATIENTS *form
an adoring group around the bath. A wreath of
leaves is held up.*]

PATIENT: [*in background*]
Marat we won't dig our own bloody graves

PATIENT: [*in background*]
Marat we've got to be clothed and fed

PATIENT: [*in background*]
Marat we're sick of working like slaves

PATIENT: [*in background*]
Marat we've got to have cheaper bread

KOKOL: [*indicating wreath*]
We crown you with these leaves Marat
because of the laurel shortage
The laurels all went to decorate

academics generals and heads of state
And their heads are enormous
> [*The wreath is placed on* MARAT's *head, he is
> lifted from the bath and carried on the shoulders
> of two patients.*]

CHORUS: Good old Marat
By your side we'll stand or fall
You're the only one that we can trust at all
> [MARAT *is carried around the arena.* SIMONNE
> *walks beside him looking up to him anxiously.
> The* FOUR SINGERS *and the* PATIENTS *in the
> procession carry out studied gestures of homage.*]

ROSSIGNOL: [*naively, taking the play seriously*]
Don't scratch your scabs or they'll never get
any better

FOUR [*Song*]
SINGERS: Four years he fought and he fought unafraid
sniffing down traitors by traitors betrayed
Marat in the courtroom Marat underground
sometimes the otter and sometimes the hound

Fighting all the gentry and fighting every priest
businessman the bourgeois the military beast
Marat always ready to stifle every scheme
of the sons of the arse-licking dying regime

We've got new generals our leaders are new
They sit and they argue and all that they do
is sell their own colleagues and ride on their
backs
and jail them and break them or give them all
the axe

Screaming in language no man understands
of rights that we grabbed with our own bleeding hands

	when we wiped out the bosses and stormed through the wall
	of the prison they told us would outlast us all
CHORUS &	Marat we're poor and the poor stay poor
FOUR	Marat don't make us wait any more
SINGERS:	We want our rights and we don't care how
	We want our revolution NOW

> [MARAT *is ceremoniously placed back in the bath. The wreath is taken from his head.*
> SIMONNE *busily changes his bandages and re-arranges the cloth about his shoulders. Music ends.*
> SADE *sits unmoving, looking across the stage with a mocking expression on his face.*]

| HERALD: | The Revolution came and went |
| | and unrest was replaced by discontent |

6. STIFLED UNREST

PATIENT:	We've got rights the right to starve
PATIENT:	We've got jobs waiting for work
PATIENT:	We're all brothers lousy and dirty
PATIENT:	We're all free and equal to die like dogs
ROSSIGNOL:	And now our lovely new leaders come
	they give us banknotes which we're told
	are money just as good as gold
	but they're only good for wiping your bum

> [COULMIER *jumps up from his seat*]

ROUX:	[*in the middle of the stage*]
	Who controls the markets
	Who locks up the granaries
	Who got the loot from the palaces
	Who sits tight on the estates
	that were going to be divided between the poor

> [COULMIER *looks around. A* SISTER *pulls* ROUX *back*]

PATIENTS: [*in the background, and beating out the rhythm emphatically*]
Who keeps us prisoner
Who locks us in
We're all normal and we want our freedom

CHORUS: Freedom Freedom Freedom
[*The unrest grows*]

COULMIER: [*knocking with his stick on the railing*]
Monsieur de Sade
[SADE *takes no notice*]
It appears I must act as the voice of reason
What's going to happen when right at the start
     of the play
the patients are so disturbed
Please keep your production under control
Times have changed times are different
and these days we should take an objective view
of old grievances
[*The* PATIENTS *are pushed back by the* MALE
NURSES.
Some SISTERS *place themselves in front of the*
PATIENTS *and sing a tranquillizing litany.*]

7. CORDAY IS INTRODUCED

[*In the middle ground* CORDAY, *who is sitting
slumped down on the bench, is being prepared
by the* SISTERS *for her entrance.*]

HERALD: Here sits Marat the people's choice
dreaming and listening to his fever's voice
You see his hand curled round his pen
and the screams from the street are all forgotten
He stares at the map of France eyes marching
     from town to town
[*Points to the map, which* MARAT *rolls up*]

	while you wait
	[*Turns round. In the background a whispering begins and spreads.*]
CHORUS:	[*whispers*]
	Corday Corday
HERALD:	while you wait for this woman to cut him down
	[*Points with his staff to* CORDAY.
	Orchestra plays the Corday theme.]
HERALD:	[*waiting for the* SISTERS *to complete their preparations*]
	And none of us
	And none of us
	[CORDAY *is led forward by the* SISTERS]
	And none of us can alter the fact do what we will
	that she stands outside his door ready and poised to kill
	[*he taps the floor three times with his staff.*
	CORDAY *is put in position in the arena.*
	This all resembles a ritual act.
	The music ends.
	The SISTERS *step back.*]
CORDAY:	[*sleepily and hesitantly*]
	Poor Marat in your bath tub
	your body soaked saturated with poison
	[*waking up*]
	Poison spurting from your hiding place
	poisoning the people
	arousing them to looting and murder
	Marat
	I have come
	I
	Charlotte Corday from Caen
	where a huge army of liberation is massing
	and Marat I come as the first of them Marat

[*Pause. A chord on the lute leads in the musical accompaniment.*]

Once both of us saw the world must go
and change as we read in great Rousseau
but change meant one thing to you I see
and something quite different to me
The very same words we both have said
to give our ideals wings to spread
    but my way was true
    while for you
the highway led over mountains of dead

Once both of us spoke a single tongue
of brotherly love we sweetly sung
but love meant one thing to you I see
and something quite different to me
but now I'm aware that I was blind
and now I can see into your mind
    and so I say no
    and I go
to murder you Marat and free all mankind
    [*Music ends.*
    CORDAY *stands with her head bowed. The* SISTERS *lead her back.*]

8. I AM THE REVOLUTION

MARAT: [*tyrannically*]
    Simonne Simonne
    More cold water
    Change my bandage
    O this itching is unbearable
        [SIMONNE *stands ready behind him and carries out with maniacal movements her rehearsed tasks. She changes his bandage, fans him with the shoulder cloth and tips a jug over the bath.*]

23

SIMONNE:	Jean-Paul don't scratch yourself
	you'll tear your skin to shreds
	give up writing Jean-Paul
	it won't do any good
MARAT:	My call
	My fourteenth of July call
	to the people of France
SIMONNE:	Jean-Paul please be more careful
	look how red the water's getting
MARAT:	And what's a bath full of blood
	compared to the bloodbaths still to come
	Once we thought a few hundred corpses would
	be enough
	then we saw thousands were still too few
	and today we can't even count all the dead
	Everywhere you look
	everywhere

> [MARAT *raises himself up in the bath.*
> *The* FOUR SINGERS *stretched out on the floor*
> *play cards, taking no notice of* MARAT.]

There they are
Behind the walls
Up on the rooftops
Down in the cellars
Hypocrites
They wear the people's cap on their heads
but their underwear's embroidered with crowns
and if so much as a shop gets looted
they squeal
Beggars villains gutter rats
Simonne Simonne
my head's on fire
I can't breathe
There is a rioting mob inside me
Simonne

24

I am the Revolution
[CORDAY *is led forward by the* SISTERS.]

9. CORDAY'S FIRST VISIT

[HERALD *taps three times with his staff on the floor and points at* CORDAY, *who is led on to the arena.*
DUPERRET *follows* CORDAY *and remains with bent knee at the edge of the arena.*
SIMONNE *stands between her and the bath.*]

HERALD: Corday's first visit
[ORCHESTRA *plays the* CORDAY *theme.*]

CORDAY: I have come to speak to Citizen Marat
I have an important message for him
about the situation in Caen my home
where his enemies are gathering

SIMONNE: We don't want any visitors
We want a bit of peace
If you've got anything to say to Marat
put it in writing

CORDAY: What I have to say cannot be said in writing
I want to stand in front of him and look at him
[*amorously*]
I want to see his body tremble and his forehead
   bubble with sweat
I want to thrust right between his ribs the
   dagger
which I carry between my breasts
[*obsessively*]
I shall take the dagger in both hands
and push it through his flesh
and then I will hear
[*approaches* MARAT]
what he has got to say to me

25

SADE:

[*She stands directly in front of the bath.*
She raised dagger and is poised to strike.
SIMONNE *stands paralysed.*
SADE *rises from his seat.*]

Not yet Corday
You have to come to his door three times
[CORDAY *stops short, hides the dagger and*
withdraws to her bench.
The SISTERS *and* DUPERRET *follow her as she*
leaves.]

10. SONG AND MIME OF CORDAY'S ARRIVAL IN PARIS

[*As an accompaniment to the song,* PATIENTS
come forward as mimes. They walk singly
around the arena. With simple disguises they
present types in the streets. One is an 'Incroyable'
another a 'Merveilleuse' or a banner-bearer, a
salesman and cutler, an acrobat or flower seller,
and there are also some prostitutes.
CORDAY *circles the arena in the opposite*
direction. She represents the country girl who has
come to town for the first time.]

FOUR
SINGERS:

[*on the edge of the arena, to a musical accompaniment.*
Song]
Charlotte Corday came to our town
heard the people talking saw the banners wave
Weariness had almost dragged her down
weariness had dragged her down

Charlotte Corday had to be brave
she could never stay at comfortable hotels
Had to find a man with knives to sell
had to find a man with knives

Charlotte Corday passed the pretty stores
Perfume and cosmetics powders and wigs
unguent for curing syphilis sores
unguent for curing your sores

She saw a dagger its handle was white
walked into the cutlery seller's door
When she saw the dagger the dagger was bright
Charlotte saw the dagger was bright

When the man asked her who is it for
it is common knowledge to each of you
Charlotte smiled and paid him his forty sous
Charlotte smiled and paid forty sous

> [*Mime of the purchase of the knife.* CORDAY *chooses the dagger, takes it and pays. She conceals the dagger under her neckcloth. The* SALESMAN *looks down her bosom with an admiring gesture.*]

Charlotte Corday walked alone
Paris birds sang sugar calls
Charlotte walked down lanes of stone
through the haze from perfume stalls
Charlotte smelt the dead's gangrene
Heard the singing guillotine

> [*The mime procession grows larger and develops into a dance of death.*
> *The* MUSIC *underlines the monotonous rhythm. Two* PATIENTS, *covered with a cloth, represent a horse. They pull a cart in which stand the condemned receiving last rites from a priest.*
> *The* PATIENTS *accompanying the cart make ecstatic and contorted movements. Some are seized with convulsions and throw themselves down in fits. One hears stifled giggles and groans and the stamping of feet to music.*]

Don't soil your pretty little shoes
The gutter's deep and red
Climb up climb up and ride along with me
the tumbrel driver said

But she never said a word
never turned her head

Don't soil your pretty little pants
I only go one way
Climb up climb up and ride along with me
There's no gold coach today

But she never said a word
never turned her head

CORDAY: [*in front of the arena, turned to the public. Behind her the stamping continues*]
What kind of town is this
The sun can hardly pierce the haze
not a haze made out of rain and fog
but steaming thick and hot
like the mist in a slaughterhouse
Why are they howling
What are they dragging through the streets
They carry stakes but what's impaled on those
    stakes
Why do they hop what are they dancing for
Why are they racked with laughter
Why do the children scream
What are those heaps they fight over
those heaps with eyes and mouths
What kind of town is this
hacked buttocks lying in the street
What are all these faces

[*Behind her the dance of death takes place.
The* FOUR SINGERS *join the dancers.*

28

The cart is turned into a place of execution. Two
PATIENTS *represent the guillotine. The execution*
is prepared in gruesome detail.
CORDAY *sits slumped at the foremost edge of the*
arena.]

Soon these faces will close around me
These eyes and mouths will call me to join them
[*The mime depicts the piercing and bursting of*
the fat belly of the priest. The condemned man
leans across the execution block. His hands are
sawn off.]

11. DEATH'S TRIUMPH

MARAT: [*speaking to the audience*]
Now it's happening and you can't stop it
  happening
The people used to suffer everything
now they take their revenge
You are watching that revenge
and you don't remember that you drove the
  people to it
Now you protest
but it's too late
to start crying over spilt blood
What is the blood of these aristocrats
compared with the blood the people shed for
  you
Many of them had their throats slit by your
  gangs
Many of them died more slowly in your
  workshops
    [*The hands of the victim fall off. Howls. The*
    executioners start sawing off his head.]
So what is this sacrifice

compared with the sacrifices the people made
to keep you fat
What are a few looted mansions
compared with their looted lives
You don't care
if the foreign armies with whom you're making
    secret deals
march in and massacre the people
You hope the people will be wiped out so you
    can flourish
and when they are wiped out not a muscle will
    twitch in your puffy bourgeois faces
which are now all twisted up with anger and
    disgust

> [COULMIER *rises. The head falls off. Trium-*
> *phant screams. The* PATIENTS *play ball with*
> *the head.*]

COULMIER: Monsieur de Sade
we can't allow this
you really cannot call this education
It isn't making my patients any better
they're all becoming over-excited
After all we invited the public here
to show them that our patients
are not all social lepers

> [SADE *does not react. He gazes with a mocking*
> *smile across the stage and cues the* HERALD.]

HERALD: [*tapping his staff before* COULMIER *has finished*
speaking]
We only show these people massacred
because this indisputably occurred
Please calmly watch these barbarous displays
which could not happen nowadays
The men of that time mostly now demised
were primitive we are more civilised

CORDAY: [*rising*]

[HERALD *points with his staff at the execution scene.*
Trumpet call.
Procession of nobles forms quickly, lining up for execution.]

CORDAY: [*rising*]
Up there on the scaffold
you stand completely still and stare
farther than your executioners can see
That is how I will stand
when it's all over
[*she closes her eyes and appears to be sleeping*]

SADE: Look at them Marat
these men who once owned everything
See how they turn their defeat into victory
Now that their pleasures have been taken away
the guillotine saves them from endless boredom
Gaily they offer their heads as if for coronation
Is not that the pinnacle of perversion
[*The victims kneel in front of the execution block.* SADE *gestures to the whole group to retreat. The* PATIENTS *withdraw. The cart is taken away.* CORDAY *is led to her bench. A curtain is drawn to hide the* PATIENTS.]

12. CONVERSATION CONCERNING LIFE AND DEATH

[*Order is restored at the back.*
The SISTERS *murmur a short litany.*]

MARAT: [*speaking to* SADE *across the empty arena*]
I read in your books de Sade
in one of your immortal works
that the animating force of Nature is destruction
and that our only instrument for measuring life
is death

31

SADE: Correct Marat
But man has given a false importance to death
Any animal plant or man who dies
adds to Nature's compost heap
becomes the manure without which
nothing could grow nothing could be created
Death is simply part of the process
Every death even the cruellest death
drowns in the total indifference of Nature
Nature herself would watch unmoved
if we destroyed the entire human race
[*rising*]
I hate Nature
this passionless spectator this unbreakable
    iceberg-face
that can bear everything
this goads us to greater and greater acts
[*breathing heavily*]
But even though I hate this goddess I see
the greatest acts in history
have followed her laws
Nature tells a man to fight for his own happi-
    ness and if he must kill to gain it
why then the murder is natural
We must reproduce we must destroy
The balance must be kept
Haven't we always beaten down those weaker
    than ourselves
Haven't we torn at their throats
with continuous villainy and lust
Haven't we experimented in our laboratories
before applying the final solution
Man is a destroyer
but if he kills and takes no pleasure in it

he is a machine
He should destroy with passion
like a man
Let me remind you of the execution of Damiens
after his unsuccessful attempt to assassinate
Louis the Fifteenth (now deceased)
Remember how Damiens died
How gentle the guillotine is
compared with his torture
It lasted four hours while the crowd goggled
and Casanova at an upper window
felt under the skirts of the ladies watching
[*pointing in the direction of the tribunal where*
COULMIER *sits*]
His chest arms thighs and calves were slit open
Molten lead was poured into each slit
boiling oil they poured over him burning tar
   wax sulphur
They burnt off his hands
tied ropes to his arms and legs
harnessed four horses to him and geed them up
They pulled at him for an hour but they'd
   never done it before
and he wouldn't come apart
until they sawed through his shoulders and hips
So he lost the first arm then the second
and he watched what they did to him and then
   turned to us
and shouted so everyone could understand
And when they tore off the first leg and then the
   second leg
he still lived though his voice was getting weak
and at the end he hung there a bloody torso
   with a nodding head
just groaning and staring at the crucifix

33

which the father confessor was holding up to
    him
[*in the background a half-murmured litany is heard*]
That
was a festival with which
today's festivals can't compete
Even our inquisition has no meaning
nowadays
Although we've only just started
there's no passion in our post-revolutionary
    murders
Now they are all official
We condemn to death without emotion
and there's no singular personal death to be had
only an anonymous cheapened death
which we could dole out to entire nations
on a mathematical basis
until the time comes
for all life
to be extinguished

MARAT: Citizen Marquis
you may have fought for us last September
when we dragged out of the gaols
the aristocrats who plotted against us
but you still talk like a grand seigneur
and what you call the indifference of Nature
is your own lack of compassion

SADE: Compassion
Now Marat you are talking like an aristocrat
Compassion is the property of the privileged
    classes
When the pitier lowers himself
to give to a beggar
he throbs with contempt
To protect his riches he pretends to be moved

and his gift to the beggar amounts to no more
    than a kick [*lute chord*]
No Marat
no small emotions please
Your feelings were never petty
For you just as for me
only the most extreme actions matter

MARAT: If I am extreme I am not extreme in the same
    way as you
Against Nature's silence I use action
In the vast indifference I invent a meaning
I don't watch unmoved I intervene
and say that this and this are wrong
and I work to alter them and improve them
The important thing
is to pull yourself up by your own hair
to turn yourself inside out
and see the whole world with fresh eyes

13. MARAT'S LITURGY

[*The curtain is drawn open.*
PATIENTS *move forward and arrange them-*
selves in a closed group.]

HERALD: Marat's liturgy
MARAT: Remember how it used to be
The kings were our dear fathers
under whose care we lived in peace
and their deeds were glorified
by official poets
Piously the simpleminded breadwinners
passed on the lesson to their children

CHORUS: [*murmuring in the background as* MARAT *continues*]
The kings are our dear fathers
under whose care we live in peace

The kings are our dear fathers
under whose care we live in peace

MARAT: And the children repeated the lesson they
believed it
as anyone believes
what they hear over and over again
    [CHORUS *repeats*]
And over and over again the priests said
    [*accompanied by chorus of* PATIENTS]
Our love embraces all mankind
of every colour race and creed
Our love is international universal
we are all brothers every one
    [*continuing alone*]
And the priests looked down into the pit of
injustice
and they turned their faces away and said
    [*accompanied by chorus of* PATIENTS]
Our kingdom is not as the kingdom of this
world
Our life on earth is but a pilgrimage
The soul lives on humility and patience
    [*continuing alone*]
at the same time screwing from the poor
their last centime
They settled down among their treasures
and ate and drank with princes
and to the starving they said
    [*accompanied by chorus of* PATIENTS]
Suffer
Suffer as he suffered on the cross
for it is the will of God
    [*A mime is performed.*
    PATIENTS *and the* FOUR SINGERS *come
    forward. Church dignitaries are depicted:*

36

CUCURUCU *carries a cross made of brooms tied*
together and leads POLPOCH *with a rope around*
his neck behind him.
KOKOL *swings a bucket as a censer.*
ROSSIGNOL *counts her beads.*]
[*Continuing alone*]

And anyone believes what they hear over and
    over again
so the poor instead of bread made do with a
    picture
of the bleeding scourged and nailed-up Christ
and prayed to that image of their helplessness
And the priests said

    [*Accompanied by chorus of* PATIENTS. *The*
    litanies of the SISTERS *can also be heard.*]

Raise your hands to heaven bend your knees
and bear your suffering without complaint
Pray for those who torture you
for prayer and blessing are the only stairways
which you can climb to Paradise
    [*speaking alone*]
And so they chained down the poor in their
    ignorance
so that they wouldn't stand up and fight their
    bosses
who ruled in the name of the lie of divine right

CHORUS: Amen
COULMIER: [*rising and calling above the Amen*]
Monsieur de Sade
I must interrupt this argument
We agreed to make some cuts in this passage
After all nobody now objects to the church
since our emperor is surrounded by high-
    ranking clergy
and since it's been proved over and over again

that the poor need the spiritual comfort of the
    priests
There's no question of anyone being oppressed
Quite on the contrary everything's done to
    relieve suffering
with clothing collections medical aid and soup
    kitchens
and in this very clinic we're dependent on the
    goodwill
not only of the temporal government
but even more on the goodness and under-
    standing of the church

HERALD: [*raising his staff*]
If our performance causes aggravation
we hope you'll swallow down your indignation
and please remember that we show
only those things which happened long ago
Remember things were very different then
of course today we're all God-fearing men
[*makes the sign of the cross*]

14. A REGRETTABLE INTERVENTION

[*A* PATIENT, *a clergyman's collar round his
neck, detaches himself from the group and hops
forward on his knees.*]

PATIENT: [*stammering incoherently*]
Pray pray
O pray to him
Our Satan which art in hell
thy kingdom come
thy will be done
on earth as it is in hell
forgive us our good deeds
and deliver us from holiness

38

Lead us
Lead us into temptation
over and over
    Amen
    [COULMIER *has sprung to his feet.*
    MALE NURSES *throw themselves on the*
    PATIENT, *overpower him, put him under a*
    shower, then bind him and drag him to the back.]

HERALD: [*swinging his rattle*]
The regrettable incident you've just seen
was unavoidable indeed foreseen
by our playwright who managed to compose
some extra lines in case the need arose
Please understand this man was once the very
well-thought-of abbot of a monastery
It should remind us all that as they say
God moves like man in a mysterious way
    [*He swings his rattle.*
    COULMIER *sits down.*
    The PATIENTS *retreat and stretch out on the*
    benches, supervised by the SISTERS *and* MALE
    NURSES.]

15. CONTINUATION OF THE CONVERSATION BETWEEN MARAT AND SADE

SADE: Before deciding what is wrong and what is right
first we must find out what we are
I
do not know myself
No sooner have I discovered something
than I begin to doubt it
and I have to destroy it again
What we do is just a shadow of what we want
    to do

and the only truths we can point to
are the ever-changing truths of our own
    experience
I do not know if I am hangman or victim
for I imagine the most horrible tortures
and as I describe them I suffer them myself
There is nothing that I could not do and every-
    thing fills me with horror
And I see that other people also
suddenly change themselves into strangers
and are driven to unpredictable acts
A little while ago I saw my tailor
a gentle cultured man who liked to talk philo-
    sophy
I saw him foam at the mouth
and raging and screaming attack with a cudgel
a man from Switzerland
a large man heavily armed
and destroy him utterly
and then I saw him
tear open the breast of the defeated man
saw him take out the still beating heart
and swallow it

> [*A* PATIENT, *in pacing across the stage, comes
> face to face with* COULMIER *and addresses part
> of his speech directly to him.*]

PATIENT: A mad animal
Man's a mad animal
I'm a thousand years old and in my time
I've helped commit a million murders
The earth is spread
The earth is spread thick
with squashed human guts
We few survivors
We few survivors

walk over a quaking bog of corpses
always under our feet
every step we take
rotted bones ashes matted hair
under our feet
broken teeth skulls split open
A mad animal
I'm a mad animal
    [SADE *comes up to him and leads him gently to*
      the back as he continues]
Prisons don't help
Chains don't help
I escape
through all the walls
through all the shit and the splintered bones
You'll see it all one day
I'm not through yet
I have plans

MARAT: [*searches for his cue*]
HERALD: [*prompting*]
O this itching
MARAT: O this itching this itching [*hesitates*]
HERALD: [*prompting*]
This fever
MARAT: This fever beats in my head like a drum
my skin simmers and scorches
Simonne
Simonne dip the cloth in vinegar and water
cool my forehead
    [SIMONNE *hastens to him and goes through her*
      motions.]
SADE: Marat I know
that you'd give up your fame and all the love of
    the people
for a few days of health

41

You lie in your bath
as if you were in the pink water of the womb
You swim all huddled up
alone with your ideas about the world
which no longer fit the world outside
And why should you care about the world
    outside
For me the only reality is imagination
the world inside myself
The Revolution
no longer interests me

MARAT: Wrong Sade wrong
This imagination you talk of is
useless to me
Imagination can't break down
any real barriers
I write but I never believed the pen alone
could destroy institutions
I know the dangers
However hard I fight for the new age
the only time it seems to come any closer
is in the quiet between our clumsy battles
We're all so clogged with dead ideas
passed from generation to generation
that even the best of us
are unable to control our own lives
We invented the Revolution
but we didn't know how to run it
Look everyone wants to keep something from
    the past
a souvenir of the old regime
    This man decides to keep a painting
    This one keeps his mistress
    This man keeps his horse
    He [*pointing*] keeps his garden

He [*pointing*] keeps his estate
He keeps his country house
He keeps his factories
This man couldn't part with his shipyards
This one kept his army
and that one keeps his king
And so we stand here
and write into the declaration of the rights of
man
the holy right of property
And now we find where that leads
Every man's equally free to fight
fraternally and with equal arms of course
Every man his own millionaire
Man against man group against group
in happy mutual robbery

[*The* PATIENTS *stand up slowly, some step
forward. The* SINGERS *take up their positions.*]

And ahead of them the great springtime of
mankind
the budding of trade and the blossoming of
industry
and one enormous financial upsurge
We stand here more oppressed than when we
begun

[*points across the auditorium*]

and they think that the revolution's been won

16. THE PEOPLE'S REACTION

THE FOUR
SINGERS:

[*With musical accompaniment.*]
Why do they have the gold
Why do they have all the power
Why do they have friends at the top
Why do they have jobs at the top

We've got nothing always had nothing
nothing but holes and millions of them

KOKOL:	Living in holes
POLPOCH:	Dying in holes
CUCURUCU:	Holes in our bellies
ROSSIGNOL:	and holes in our clothes

THE FOUR   Marat we're poor and the poor stay poor
SINGERS &   Marat don't make us wait any more
CHORUS: We want our rights and we don't care how
We want our Revolution NOW

HERALD: [*coming forward quickly, swinging his staff. Music
ends. The* FOUR SINGERS *and* CHORUS *withdraw*]
Observe how easily a crowd turns mob
through ignorance of its wise ruler's job
Rather than bang an empty drum
of protest citizens be dumb
Work for and trust the powerful few
what's best for them is best for you
Ladies and gentlemen we'd like to see
people and government in harmony
a harmony which I should say
we've very nearly reached today

[DUPERRET *and the* SISTERS *busy themselves
with* CORDAY, *who cannot be awakened. They
pull her to her feet and hold her up and try to
get her moving.*]

17. FIRST CONVERSATION BETWEEN CORDAY
AND DUPERRET

[CORDAY *is led forward by the two* SISTERS,
supporting her under the arms.
DUPERRET   *walks   behind,   supporting*
CORDAY's *back with his hands.*]

HERALD: [*plays a few runs on his Pan-flute*]

44

And now nobility meets grace
Our author brings them face to face
The beautiful and brave Charlotte Corday
[*turns round in concern, nods in relief and points his
staff at* CORDAY]
The handsome Monsieur Duperret

> [*With the help of the* SISTERS, CORDAY *enters
> the arena.* DUPERRET *walks beside her.*
> *The* SISTERS *withdraw.*
> CORDAY *and* DUPERRET *greet each other with
> exaggerated ceremony.*]

In Caen where she spent the best years of her
    youth
in a convent devoted to the way of truth
Duperret's name she heard them recommend
as a most sympathetic helpful friend

> [DUPERRET *uses the scene to make amorous
> advances to* CORDAY.
> *The* HERALD *addresses* DUPERRET.]

Confine your passion to the lady's mind
Your love's platonic not the other kind

> [*He gives the* ORCHESTRA *a sign with his staff.*
> CORDAY *stands with head held back, eyes
> closed.*
> *The* ORCHESTRA *plays the Corday theme.*
> *The* HERALD *withdraws. He waits a few
> seconds and watches* CORDAY.]

CORDAY: [*with her eyes closed*]
Ah dearest Duperret
[*she hesitates then starts again as if singing an aria*]
Ah dearest Duperret what can we do
How can we stop this dreadful calamity
In the streets everyone is saying
Marat's to be

45

[*She hesitates.*

DUPERRET *gently caresses her hips and back.*]
Marat's to be tribune and dictator
He still pretends that his iron grip
will relax as soon as the worst is over
But we know what Marat really wants
anarchy and confusion
[CORDAY *stands sunk into herself.*]

DUPERRET: [*embracing* CORDAY, *also as if singing an aria, but with great ardour*]
Dearest Charlotte you must return
return to your friends the pious nuns
and live in prayer and contemplation
You cannot fight
the hard-faced enemies surrounding us
[*One of the* SISTERS *approaches* DUPERRET *and pulls back his hand, which he had placed on her bosom.*

CORDAY *stands sunk into herself.*]
You talk about Marat but who's this Marat
A street salesman a funfair barker
a layabout from Corsica sorry I mean Sardinia
Marat the name sounds Jewish to me
perhaps derived from the waters of Marah in the Bible
But who listens to him
Only the mob down in the streets
Up here Marat can be no danger to us
[DUPERRET *embraces* CORDAY'S *hips.*

The FOUR SINGERS *are filling in time with all sorts of pranks, throwing dice and showing each other card tricks.*]

CORDAY: [*suddenly awake and full of power*]
Dearest Duperret you're trying to test me

but I know what I must do
[*tries to free herself from* DUPERRET's *embrace. The two* SISTERS *standing behind the podium interfere and pull back* DUPERRET's *hands.*]
Duperret go to Caen
Barbaroux and Buzot are waiting for you there
Go now and travel quickly
Do not wait till this evening
for this evening everything will be too late

DUPERRET: [*passionately, in aria style as before*]
Dearest Charlotte my place is here
[*throws himself on his knees and hugs her legs*]
How could I leave the city which holds you
Dearest Charlotte
my place is here
[*he forgets himself and becomes wilder in his embracing. The* HERALD *pushes him with his staff and then taps on the floor.*]

HERALD: [*prompting*]
And why should I run

DUPERRET: And why should I run
now when it can't last much longer
[*stroking* CORDAY *vigorously*]
Already the English lie off Dunkirk and Toulon
The Prussians

HERALD: [*prompting*]
The Spaniards

DUPERRET: The Spaniards have occupied Roussillon
Paris

HERALD: [*prompting*]
Mayence

DUPERRET: Mayence is surrounded by the Prussians
Condé and Valenciennes have fallen to the
Russians

47

HERALD: [*correcting*]
               Austrians

DUPERRET: To the Austrians
               The Vendée is up in arms
               [*with much ardour and vigorous embraces*]
               They can't hold out much longer
               these fanatical upstarts
               with no vision and no culture
               They can't hold out much longer
               No dear Charlotte here I stay
               [*snuggles up to her and puts his head into her lap*]
               waiting for the promised day
               when with Marat's mob interred
               France once more speaks the forbidden word
               Freedom

                    [DUPERRET *raises himself, clinging to*
                    CORDAY, *tries to kiss her.*
                    CORDAY *extricates herself, the two* SISTERS
                    come to her aid, pushing DUPERRET *away and
                    pulling her back to her bench.*
                    The MUSIC *ends.*]

18. SADE TURNS HIS BACK ON ALL THE NATIONS

SADE: [*shouting to* MARAT]
               You hear that Marat
               Freedom
               They all say they want what's best for France
               My patriotism's bigger than yours
               They're all ready to die for the honour of
                    France
               Radical or moderate
               they're all after the taste of blood

                           [*rising*]
The luke-warm liberals and the angry radicals
all believe in the greatness of France
Marat
can't you see this patriotism is lunacy
Long ago I left heroics to the heroes
and I care no more for this country
than for any other country

COULMIER: [*calling over them with raised forefinger*]
Take care

PATIENT: [*in the background*]
Long live Napoleon and the nation
[*a shrill laugh in the background*]

KOKOL: [*at back calling*]
Long live all emperors kings bishops and popes
[*signs of disorder in the background*]

POLPOCH: Long live watery broth and the straitjacket

ROSSIGNOL: Long live Marat

ROUX: Long live the Revolution
[*shouting above the disorder*]

SADE: It's easy to get mass movements going
movements that move in vicious circles
        [*Shrill whistles in background.*
        A PATIENT *begins to run in a circle, a second*
        and third join in.
        MALE NURSES pursue them and halt them.]

SADE: I don't believe in idealists
who charge down blind alleys
I don't believe in any of the sacrifices
that have been made for any cause
I believe only in myself

MARAT: [*turning violently to* SADE]
I believe in the Revolution
We've overthrown our wealthy rabble of rulers
disarmed many of them though

many escaped
But now those rulers have been replaced by
    others
who used to carry torches and banners with us
and now long for the good old days
It becomes clear
that the Revolution was fought
for merchants and shopkeepers
the bourgeoisie
a new victorious class
and underneath them
ourselves
who always lose the lottery

FOUR
SINGERS:
    Those fat monkeys covered in banknotes
have champagne and brandy on tap
They're up to their eyeballs in franc notes
We're up to our noses in crap

Those gorilla-mouthed fakers
are longing to see us all rot
The gentry may lose a few acres
but we lose the little we've got

Revolution it's more like a ruin
They're all stuffed with glorious food
They think about nothing but screwing
but we are the ones who get screwed

19. FIRST RABBLE-ROUSING OF JACQUES ROUX

ROUX:
    [*springing on a bench in background, shouting*]
Pick up your arms
Fight for your rights
Grab what you need and grab it now
or wait a hundred years
and see what the authorities arrange

50

[PATIENTS *approach* ROUX *from the tribunal*]
Up there they despise you
because you never had the cash
to learn to read and write
You're good enough for the dirty work of the
    Revolution
but they screw their noses up at you
because your sweat stinks
You have to sit way down there
so they won't have to see you
And down there
in ignorance and stink
you're allowed to do your bit
towards bringing in the golden age
in which you'll all do the same old dirty work
Up there in the sunlight
their poets sing
about the power of life
and the expensive rooms in which they scheme
are hung with exquisite paintings
So stand up
Defend yourselves from their whips
Stand up stand in front of them
and let them see how many of you there are
    [*The* FOUR SINGERS *sit down in the arena and*
    pass a bottle around.
    The two SISTERS *grab* ROUX *from behind and*
    pull him down from the dais.]

COULMIER: [*springing up*]
Do we have to listen to this sort of thing
We're citizens of a new enlightened age
We're all revolutionaries nowadays
but this is plain treachery we can't allow it

HERALD: [*sounding a shrill whistle*]
The cleric you've been listening to

is that notorious priest Jacques Roux
[*points with his staff at* ROUX]
who to adopt the new religious fashion
has quit the pulpit and with earthier passion
rages from soapboxes A well-trained priest
his rhetoric is slick to say the least
'If you'd make paradise your only chance
is not to build on clouds but solid France'
The mob eats from his hand while Roux
knows what he wants but not what he should do
Talk's cheap The price of action is colossal
so Roux decides to be the chief apostle
of Jean-Paul Marat Seems good policy
since Marat's heading straight for Calvary
and crucifixion all good Christians know
is the most sympathetic way to go

ROUX: [*frees himself and jumps forward*]
We demand
the opening of the granaries to feed the poor
We demand
the public ownership of workshops and factories
    [*The* FOUR SINGERS *listen to the disturbance,*
    but soon lose interest. They quarrel for the last
    drop of the bottle.]
We demand
the conversion of the churches into schools
so that now at last something useful can be
   taught in them
    [COULMIER *wrings his hands and signifies*
    protest]
We demand that everyone should do all they
   can
to put an end to war
This damned war
which is run for the benefit of profiteers

and leads only to more wars
> [COULMIER *runs across to* SADE *and speaks to him, but* SADE *does not react.*]

We demand
that the people who started the war
should pay the cost of it
> [*The* FOUR SINGERS *continue their antics.*]

Once and for all
the idea of glorious victories
won by the glorious army
must be wiped out
Neither side is glorious
On either side they're just frightened men
    messing their pants
and they all want the same thing
Not to lie under the earth
but to walk upon it
without crutches

COULMIER: [*shouting over him*]
This is outright pacifism
At this very moment our soldiers are laying
    down their lives
for the freedom of the world and for our
    freedom
[*turning violently to* SADE]
This scene was cut

SADE: [*calling out, without concerning himself with* COULMIER'*s protest*]
Bravo Jacques Roux
I like your monk's habit
Nowadays it's best
to preach revolution
wearing a robe
> [ROUX *is overpowered by the two* NURSES *and dragged off.* DUPERRET *makes violent passes at*

CORDAY *who remains impassive. The* PATIENTS *come forward restlessly.*]

ROUX: [*as he is being strapped to a bench*]
Marat
Your hour has come
Now Marat show yourself
Come out and lead the people
They are waiting for you
It must be now
For the Revolution
which burns up everything
in blinding brightness
will only last as long as a lightning flash

20. MONSIEUR DE SADE IS WHIPPED

[ROUX *jumps up, the bench strapped to his back. He is overpowered.*
The PATIENTS *are pushed back.*
SADE *comes slowly into the arena. He speaks without bothering about the noise.*]

SADE: Marat
Today they need you because you are going to suffer for them
They need you and they honour the urn which holds your ashes
Tomorrow they will come back and smash that urn
and they will ask
Marat who was Marat
Marat
Now I will tell you
what I think of this revolution
which I helped to make
[*It has become very quiet in the background.*]

When I lay in the Bastille
my ideas were already formed
I sweated them out
under the blows of my own whip
out of hatred for myself
and the limitations of my mind
In prison I created in my mind
monstrous representatives of a dying class
who could still exercise their power
in spectacularly staged orgies
I recorded the mechanics of their atrocities
in the minutest detail
and brought out everything wicked and brutal
that lay inside me
In a criminal society
I dug the criminal out of myself
so I could understand him and so understand
the times we live in
My imaginary giants committed
desecrations and tortures
I committed them myself
and like them allowed myself to be bound and
    beaten
And even now I should like to take
this beauty here
    [*pointing to* CORDAY, *who is brought forward*]
who stands there so expectantly
and let her beat me
while I talk to you about the Revolution
    [*The* SISTERS *place* CORDAY *in the arena.*
    SADE *hands her a many-stranded whip. He*
    tears off his shirt and offers his back to
    CORDAY. *He stands facing the audience.*
    CORDAY *stands behind him. The* PATIENTS
    advance slowly from the background. The ladies

55

on Coulmier's dais stand up expectantly.]
At first I saw in the revolution a chance
for a tremendous outburst of revenge
an orgy greater than all my dreams
          [CORDAY *slowly raises the whip and lashes him.*
          SADE *cowers.*]
But then I saw
when I sat in the courtroom myself
          [*Whiplash.* SADE *gasps.*]
not as I had been before the accused
but as a judge
I couldn't bring myself
to deliver the prisoner to the hangman
          [*Whiplash.*]
I did all I could to release him or let him escape
I saw I wasn't capable of murder
          [*Whiplash.* SADE *groans asthmatically.*]
although murder
was the final proof of my existence
and now
          [*Whiplash. He gasps and groans.*]
the very thought of it
horrifies me
In September when I saw
the official sacking of the Carmelite Convent
I had to bend over in the courtyard
and vomit
          [CORDAY *stops, herself breathing heavily.*]
as I saw my own prophecies coming true
          [*He falls down on his knees.* CORDAY *stands
          before him.*]
and women running by
holding in their dripping hands
the severed genitals of men

[CORDAY *flogs him again. He groans and falls
forward.*]
And then in the next few months
[*hindered by his asthma*]
as the tumbrels ran regularly to the scaffolds
and the blade dropped and was winched up
and dropped again
[*Whiplash.*]
all the meaning drained out of this revenge
It had become mechanical
[*Another blow. He crumples.* CORDAY *stands
very erect.*]
It was inhuman it was dull
and curiously technocratic
[*Whiplash.*]
And now Marat
[*Whiplash.* SADE *breathes heavily.*]
now I see where
this revolution is leading
[CORDAY *stands breathlessly, holding the whip
over* SADE. *The two* SISTERS *move forward and
pull her back. She does not resist, dragging the
whip behind her.* SADE *continues, lying on his
knees.*]
To the withering of the individual man
and a slow merging into uniformity
to the death of choice
to self denial
to deadly weakness
in a state
which has no contact with individuals
but which is impregnable
So I turn away
I am one of those who has to be defeated
and from this defeat I want to seize

57

all I can get with my own strength
I step out of my place
and watch what happens
without joining in
observing
noting down my observations
and all around me
stillness
[*pauses, breathing heavily*]
And when I vanish
I want all trace of my existence
to be wiped out
> [*He takes his shirt and returns to his chair,
> slowly dressing.*]

21. POOR OLD MARAT

MARAT: [*bent forward, sunk into himself*]
Simonne Simonne
[*staring as if blind*]
Why is it getting so dark
Give me a fresh cloth for my forehead
Put a new towel round my shoulders
I don't know
if I am freezing or burning to death
> [SIMONNE *stands ready and bends over him with
> her jerky movements, puts a hand to his brow,
> changes the cloths, fans him. The* PATIENTS
> *cower behind the arena.*]

Simonne
Fetch Bas so I can dictate my call
my call to the people of France
> [SIMONNE *shakes her head in horror and puts a
> hand over her mouth.*]

Simonne

Where are my papers
I saw them only a moment ago
Why is it so dark

SIMONNE: [*pushing the papers lying on the board nearer*]
They're here can't you see Jean-Paul

MARAT: Where's the ink
Where's my pen

SIMONNE: [*indicating*]
Here's your pen Jean-Paul
and here's the ink
where it always is
That was only a cloud over the sun
or perhaps smoke
They are burning the corpses

    [*The* ORCHESTRA *plays. The* FOUR SINGERS
    come forward.]

FOUR
SINGERS: [*singing to music*]
Poor old Marat they hunt you down
The bloodhounds are sniffing all over the town
Just yesterday your printing press
was smashed Now they're asking your home
    address

Poor old Marat in you we trust
You work till your eyes turn as red as rust
but while you write they're on your track
The boots mount the staircase the door's flung
    back
[*together with* CHORUS]
Marat we're poor and the poor stay poor
Marat don't make us wait any more
We want our rights and we don't care how
We want our Revolution NOW

    [*Music Finale.* SINGERS *withdraw. The*
    PATIENTS *close the curtain.*]

22. SECOND CONVERSATION BETWEEN CORDAY AND DUPERRET

> [*The* SISTERS *and* DUPERRET *busy themselves with* CORDAY. *Together they raise her up. The* SISTERS *arrange her clothes and tie on her hat. The* HERALD *comes forward and knocks his staff on the floor three times.*]

HERALD: [*plays a few runs on his Pan-flute*]

Now that these painful matters have been
    clarified
let's turn and look upon the sunny side
Fever sores death not one of them destroys
the universal rule of love's sweet joys
Anger and woe don't give a true reflection
of life there's also spiritual affection
Recall this couple and their love so pure

> [CORDAY *is led to the centre by* SISTERS. DUPERRET *has his arm around her.*
> *The* HERALD *points his staff*]

she with her neatly-groomed coiffure

> [*points to it*]

and her face intriguingly pale and clear

> [*points to it*]

and her eyes ashine with the trace of a tear

> [*points to them*]

her lips sensual and ripe seeming to silently cry
    for protection

> [*points to them*]

and his embraces proving his affection

> [*Points to* DUPERRET, *who lifts* CORDAY's *foot and kisses her shoe, then covers her leg in kisses.* CORDAY *pushes him back.*]

See how he moves with natural grace

[DUPERRET *loses his balance and, without grace, sits on his behind, but rises immediately and strikes a comic amorous pose before* CORDAY, *who turns her face from him in disgust.*]

and how his heart sprints on at passion's pace
[*points to* DUPERRET's *breast*]
Let's gaze at the sweet blending of the strong
    and fair sex
before their heads fall off their necks

    [ORCHESTRA *plays* CORDAY *theme.* She
    hesitates, looking for her words.
    The HERALD *prompts her.*]

HERALD: One day it will come to pass

CORDAY: [*in the aria style*]
    One day it will come to pass
    Man will live in harmony with himself
    and with his fellow-man

DUPERRET: [*covers her hand and arm with kisses*]
      One day it will come
    [*he strokes her hair, singing in the aria style*]
    a society which will pool its energy
    to defend and protect
    each person for the possession of each person
    and in which each individual
    although united with all the others
    [*putting a hand under* CORDAY's *dress.* She *defends
    herself.*]
    only obeys himself
    and so stays free

    [DUPERRET *tries to kiss* CORDAY's *mouth.*
    She *avoids him.*]

CORDAY: A society
    in which every man is trusted with the right
    of governing himself himself

DUPERRET: [*holding* CORDAY *and embracing her violently*]
One day it will come
a constitution in which the natural inequalities
    of man
        [CORDAY *leans back.* DUPERRET *jumps after
        her, continuing*]
are subject to a higher order
[*breathless*]
so that all
        [*One of the* SISTERS *gets hold of* CORDAY *and
        leads her back.* CORDAY *is placed in a heroic
        pose.*]
however varied their physical and mental
    powers may be
by agreement legally
get their fair share
        [*He utters a sigh of relief, and then he also falls
        into a suitable pose so that they form a pleasant
        tableau.*]

23. THESE LIES THEY TELL

        [MARAT *raises himself up.* CORDAY *is led
        back by the* SISTERS. DUPERRET *follows her.*]
MARAT: These lies they tell about the ideal state
The rich will never give away their property
of their own free will
And if by force of circumstances
they have to give up just a little
here and there
they do it only because they know
they'll soon win it back again
The rumour spreads
that the workers can soon expect higher wages
Why

[*The head of a* PATIENT *appears from behind
the curtain, which is opened from inside.*]

Because this raises production and increases
  demand

to fill the rich man's gold-chest

Don't imagine

that you can beat them without using force

[*The* PATIENTS *rise one by one and advance
slowly, listening intently.*

CORDAY *lies stretched out on the dais,*
DUPERRET *leans over her.*]

Don't be deceived

when our Revolution has been finally stamped
  out

and they tell you

things are better now

Even if there's no poverty to be seen

because the poverty's been hidden

even if you ever got more wages

and could afford to buy

more of these new and useless goods

which these new industries foist on you

and even if it seems to you

that you never had so much

that is only the slogan of those

who still have much more than you

[*The* PATIENTS *and* FOUR SINGERS *advance
slowly.*]

Don't be taken in

when they pat you paternally on the shoulder
  and say

that there's no inequality worth speaking of

and no more reason

for fighting

[COULMIER *looks around, worried.*]

Because if you believe them
[*turns towards the audience*]
they will be completely in charge
in their marble homes and granite banks
from which they rob the people of the world
under the pretence of bringing them culture

> [COULMIER *leaves the platform and hurries
> towards* SADE. *He speaks to him.* SADE *does
> not react.*]

Watch out
for as soon as it pleases them
they'll send you out
to protect their gold
in wars

> [SADE *rises and moves to the arena.*]

whose weapons rapidly developed
by servile scientists
will become more and more deadly
until they can with a flick of a finger
tear a million of you to pieces

SADE: Lying there
scratched and swollen
your brow burning

> [COULMIER *nods with satisfaction and returns
> to the platform.*]

in your world your bath
you still believe that justice is possible
you still believe all men are equal
Do you still believe that all occupations
are equally valuable equally satisfying
and that no man wants to be greater than the
    others
How does the old song go

24. SONG AND MIME OF THE GLORIFICATION OF THE BENEFICIARY

> [*The* FOUR SINGERS *perform a mime, in which they illustrate the cash value of all the things* SADE *names.*]

SADE:
One always bakes the most delicate cakes
Two is the really superb masseur
Three sets your hair with exceptional flair
Four's brandy goes to the Emperor
Five knows each trick of advanced rhetoric
Six bred a beautiful brand-new rose
Seven can cook every dish in the book
And eight cuts you flawlessly elegant clothes
Do you think those eight would be happy
if each of them could climb so high
and no higher
before banging their heads on equality
if each could be only a small link
in a long and heavy chain
Do you still think it's possible
to unite mankind
when already you see how the few idealists
who did join together in the name of harmony
are now out of tune
and would like to kill each other over trifles

MARAT:
[*raising himself*]
But they aren't trifles
They are matters of principle
and it's usual in a revolution
for the half-hearted and the fellow-travellers
to be dropped

> [*Mime ends.* MARAT *stands up in the bath.*]

We can't begin to build till we've burnt the old
  building down

65

however dreadful that may seem to those
who lounge in make-believe contentment
wearing their scruples as protective clothing
Listen
Can you hear through the walls
how they plot and whisper

> [MARAT *gets out of the bath and stumbles
> around the arena as if about to faint. Some
> nurses seize him and put him back into the
> bath.*]

Do you see how they lurk everywhere
waiting for the chance to strike

THE FOUR
SINGERS:
[*to music accompaniment, singly, speaking in con-
versational tones while promenading*]
What has gone wrong with
the men who are ruling
I'd like to know who
they think they are fooling
They told us that torture
was over and gone
but everyone knows
the same torture goes on
The king's gone away
The priests emigrating
The nobles are buried
so why are we waiting

25. CORDAY'S SECOND VISIT

> [CORDAY *is prepared by the* SISTERS *who lead
> her forward.* DUPERRET *follows them.* MARAT
> sits waiting in his bath. SIMONNE *changes his
> cloths.* SADE *stands in front of his chair.*
> CORDAY *is placed on the arena in a pose. She
> holds up her hand as if about to knock. The*

SISTERS *stand behind her ready to support her.*
DUPERRET *sits down. The* FOUR SINGERS
stop in front of the musicians.

The HERALD *gives* CORDAY *a sign with his
staff, she moves her hand as if knocking, and the*
HERALD *knocks three times with his staff on
the floor.*

The ORCHESTRA *plays the* CORDAY *theme.*]

HERALD: Now Charlotte Corday stands outside
Marat's front door the second time she's tried
[*points to* CORDAY. SIMONNE *straightens and goes a
few steps towards* CORDAY.]

CORDAY: [*quietly*]
I have come
to deliver this letter
[*draws a letter from her bodice*]
in which I ask again
to be received by Marat
[*hesitates*]
I am unhappy
and therefore have a right to his aid
[CORDAY *holds the letter out to* SIMONNE.
SIMONNE, *confused, takes a step towards*
CORDAY, *returns to the back and begins to
change* MARAT's *bandage.*]

CORDAY: [*repeating loudly*]
I have a right to his aid
[*She stretches out her hand.* SIMONNE *wavers
nervously about, then runs to* CORDAY *and
snatches the letter from her.*]

MARAT: Who was that at the door Simonne
[SIMONNE *hesitates in confusion between*
CORDAY *and* MARAT.]

HERALD: [*prompting*]

67

A girl from Caen with a letter
a petitioner

> [CORDAY *is now standing sunk into herself.*
> DUPERRET *rises and puts his arm around her*
> *waist.*
>
> *The two* SISTERS *come up.* CORDAY *is led off.*]

SIMONNE: [*confused and angry*]

I won't let anyone in
They only bring us trouble
All these people with their convulsions and
    complaints
As if you had nothing better to do
than be their lawyer and doctor and confessor

> [*She tears the letter up and puts the pieces in her*
> *apron. She puts a fresh cloth around* MARAT'*s*
> *shoulders.*]

SADE: [*goes into the arena and stops near the bath. Musical*
accompaniment.]

That's how it is Marat
That's how she sees your revolution
They have toothache
and their teeth should be pulled

> [*The* FOUR SINGERS *mime the characters in his*
> *speech. They mime very slowly, with economical*
> *gestures illustrating suffering.*]

Their soup's burnt
they shout for better soup
A woman finds her husband too short
she wants a taller one
A man finds his wife too skinny
he wants a plumper one
A man's shoes pinch
but his neighbour's shoes fit comfortably
A poet runs out of poetry
and desperately gropes for new images

68

For hours an angler casts his line
Why aren't the fish biting
And so they join the revolution
thinking the revolution will give them every-
    thing
a fish
a poem
a new pair of shoes
a new wife
a new husband
and the best soup in the world
So they storm all the citadels
and there they are
and everything is just the same
no fish biting
verses botched
shoes pinching
a worn and stinking partner in bed
and the soup burnt
and all that heroism
which drove us down to the sewers
well we can talk about it to our grandchildren
if we have any grandchildren
        [MUSIC *changes to a quartet with tragic
        flavour.*]

THE FOUR   [*taking up their positions*]
SINGERS: Marat Marat it's all in vain
                You studied the body and probed the brain
                In vain you spent your energies
                for how can Marat cure his own disease

                Marat Marat where is our path
                or is it not visible from your bath
                Your enemies are closing in
                Without you the people can never win

[MARAT *lays himself wearily across the board.*]
Marat Marat can you explain
how once in the daylight your thought seemed
    plain
Has your affliction left you dumb
Your thoughts lie in shadows now night has
    come

[*The music changes to a dramatic growling.*
MARAT *is in a fever.* SIMONNE *feels his brow,*
fans him, changes his bandage.]

26. THE FACES OF MARAT

[*The whole stage trembles and roars. The*
mimes appear with a cart. The cart is drawn by
a man and a woman who represent MARAT'S
parents. The characters in the cart stand for
Science, the Army, the Church, the Nouveaux
Riches. The priest blesses the owner of the
sack of gold looted from the aristocrats. The
figures are bedecked with medals and with
primitive insignia. The costumes are extremely
grotesque.]

MARAT: [*raising himself up*]
They are coming
Listen to them
and look carefully at
these gathering figures
Listen closely
Watch
Yes I hear you
all the voices I ever heard
Yes I see you
all the old faces
[*the loud noise continues*]

HERALD: [*tapping his staff*]
Ladies and gentlemen silence I pray
Let's hear what these people are aching to say
[*pointing to figures*]
about this man
[*pointing to* MARAT]
whom they all understood
before they bury him for good
First the schoolmaster of that charming place
[*points to schoolmaster*]
in which this man
[*points to* MARAT]
spent his childhood days

SCHOOL-
MASTER: [*sings in a falsetto voice*]
Even as a child
this Marat
made groups of his friends
rush screaming at each other
they fought with wooden swords
but real blood flowed
[*cries are heard in the background*]
and they took prisoners
and bound and tortured them
and nobody knew why

HERALD: [*pointing to the figure representing* MARAT's *mother*]
Now let us hear this lady for she can
give us the inside story of this man
She smelt him from the very first
for from her womb young Marat burst

MOTHER: [*in a complaining voice*]
Wouldn't eat his food
Lay around for days saying nothing
Broke a lot of canes on his hide we did
[*she laughs shrilly. Laughter is heard in the back-
ground, also the sound of whipping.*]

71

Locked him up in the cellar of course
but nothing helped
There was no getting at him
Oh
[*she starts laughing again*]

FATHER: [*springing forward, in a hurried voice*]
When I bit him he bit back
his own father
Threw himself down when I wanted to hang
him up
and when I spat at him he lay there stiff as a
poker
cold as ice
[*starts to laugh harshly*]

MARAT: Yes I see you
hated father hated mother
[*The two figures squat down, still shaking with
laughter. They rock to and fro as if sitting in a
boat.*]
What's that boat you're rocking in
I see you
I hear you
Why do you laugh like executioners
[*The two figures sit rocking, their laughter dies.*]

SIMONNE: [*approaching the bath*]
Jean-Paul you're feverish
Stop writing Jean-Paul
or it'll kill you
Lie still
You must take more care of yourself

MARAT: I'm not feverish
Now I see clearly
those figures were always hallucinations
Why doesn't Bas come
Fetch him

	My call to the nation
	I must write my call
	Bas
SCHOOL- MASTER:	[*jumping forward*]
	When he was five this loudmouth boasted
	I can do anything teacher can do
	and what's more I know more
	and at fifteen I've conquered the uni-v-v-v- versities
	and outdone all the p-p-professors
	and at the age of twenty I've mastered
	the entire in-in-in-intellectual cosmos
	That's what he boasted
	as true as I stand here
	[*swings his cane*]
MARAT:	Simonne
	where are my old manuscripts
	My novel about the young Count Potovsky
	and my book about the chains of slavery
SIMONNE:	[*defensively*]
	Leave all that stuff
	It'll only bring you trouble
MARAT:	[*raising himself up*]
	I want to see them
	Look for them
	bring them to me
SCHOOL- MASTER:	Scribblings of a pickpocket
	pilfered thoughts
	frivolities tirades
MILITARY REPRESENT- ATIVE:	One book published under the name of a count
	The other under the name of a prince
	Just look at him
	this charlatan
	greedy for titles and court distinctions
	who turned on those he once flattered

only because they did not recognise him

A Scientist: What did he do in England this shady Marat
Wasn't he a dandy in the highest society
who had to run away
because he was caught red-handed embezzling
and stealing
Didn't he smuggle himself back into well-
known circles
and get himself appointed physician
to the Count d'Artois
or was it only to his horses
Didn't we see him going about with aristocrats
He charged thirty-six livres for a consultation
and on top of that enjoyed the favours of
certain well-born ladies
[Coulmier's *wife and daughter applaud.*]

A Newly
Rich: And when at last they let him drop
back to his kind the simple poor
and when he spoke and couldn't stop
each word from branding him a boor
and when they found he was a quack
with watered drugs and pills of chalk
and when they threw him on his back
He raised his battered head to squawk
Property is Robbery
[*cries in the background*]
Down with all Tyrants
[*the cry is taken up in the background*]

Marat: Bas fetch Bas
[Voltaire *emerges from the darkness, suitably
masked and with corkscrew curls.*]

Chorus: Bas

Herald: [*as* Voltaire *advances*]
It is a privilege indeed
to introduce Voltaire He wrote Candide

74

VOLTAIRE: [*monotonously*]
             We have received from a certain Marat
             a slim volume
             entitled Man
             This Marat claims in a somewhat revolutionary
                 essay
             that the soul exists in the walls of the brain
             and from that strategic point controls
             the hypodraulic mechanism of the body
             by means of a network of tinkling nerve threads
             At the same time apparently the soul is
                 receiving
             messages from the mechanamism of the body
             messages conveyed by pistons plugs and wires
             which the soul transforms into consciousness
                 through separate
             centimentrifuges operating asimultaneously
             In other words
             it is the opinion of this gentleman
             that a corn fills the corridors of the brain with
                 the essence of the soul
             and that a troubled soul curdles the liver and
             kidneys
             For this kind of ring-a-ring-a-roses
             we can spare not even our laughter
                     [CUCURUCU *and* ROSSIGNOL *laugh ironically*
                     Ha Ha Ha. A figure with a palm branch moves
                     forward.]

HERALD: We're equally happy to welcome today
             that eminent scientist Lavoisier
             [*points to him*]

LAVOISIER: [*monotonously*]
             The Academy has received from a certain
                 Marat

                             75

some theories concerning fire light and
electricity
This Marat seems entirely certain
that he knows a great deal better than the
Academy
For fire he says is not an element
but a liquid fluidium caused by heat
which only ignites because of air
Light he proceeds to say is not light
but a path of vibratorating rays
left behind by light
Certainly an extraordinary scientist
He goes further
Heat according to him is not of course heat
but simply more vibratoratory rays
which become heat only
when they collide with a body and set in
motionability
its miniscule molecules
He wants to pronounce
the whole of firm and fixed creation
invalid
And instead he wants to introduce
a universe of unbridled activation
in which electrified magnetic forces
whizz about and rub against each other
No wonder that the author sits there in his bath
attempting to determine the validity of the
proposition
The more you scratch the more you itch

> [KOKOL and POLPOCH laugh ironically Ha Ha
> Ha. FATHER and MOTHER join in the laughter.
> The figures mime the attitude of judges about
> to give a verdict.]

VOLTAIRE:	So this frustrated Newton's eyes
PRIEST:	turned to the streets He thought it best
SCHOOL-M:	to join the revolutionaries
NEWLY RICH:	and beat his dilettante breast
PRIEST:	crying out The oppressed must rise
LAVOISIER:	He meant of course I am oppressed

[*Rocking to and fro and laughing the* FATHER *and* MOTHER *pull back the cart with the figures.* ROUX *hurries to the front, a belated advocate.*]

ROUX:
Woe to the man who is different
who tries to break down all the barriers
Woe to the man
who tries to stretch the imagination of man
He shall be mocked he shall be scourged
by the blinkered guardians of morality
You wanted enlightenment and warmth
and so you studied light and heat
[*unrest in background*]
You wondered how forces can be controlled
so you studied electricity
You wanted to know what man is for
so you asked yourself What is this soul
this dump for hollow ideals and mangled morals
You decided that the soul is in the brain
      [*The* PATIENTS *form into a group and advance.*]
and that it can learn to think
For to you the soul is a practical thing
a tool for ruling and mastering life
And you came one day to the Revolution
because you saw the most important vision
That our circumstances must be changed
   fundamentally
and without these changes
everything we try to do must fail

77

[COULMIER *jumps up. The* SISTERS *and* MALE
NURSES *run towards* ROUX *and pull him into
the background.* SADE *stands erect in front of his
chair and smiles.* CORDAY *lies sleeping on her
bench.* DUPERRET *sits by her on the floor.*]

CHORUS: [*to music while the* SISTERS *sing a litany*]
Marat we're poor and the poor stay poor
Marat don't make us wait any more
We want our rights and we don't care how
We want our Revolution NOW [*music ends*]

HERALD: [*swinging his rattle*]
The end comes soon Before we watch the crime
let's interpose a drinking thinking time
while you recall that what our cast presents
is simply this a series of events
but that our end which might seem pre-
arranged
could be delayed or even changed
We will since it's a play not actual history
postpone it with an interval We guarantee
that after your refreshments and debating
you'll find Marat still in his bathtub waiting
[*points to* MARAT]

CURTAIN

ACT TWO

[The handbell is rung behind the curtain. Curtain goes up.]

27. THE NATIONAL ASSEMBLY

[The setting is the same, but with the following changes:

DUPERRET sits on the steps leading to SADE's raised chair, between the two PATIENTS representing prostitutes. On the left are seated the PATIENTS who represent the Girondists in the National Assembly.

SADE stands underneath COULMIER's platform. The bath has been removed from MARAT's dais. On it are the FOUR SINGERS and the PATIENTS who represent the Jacobites. PATIENTS sit on benches alongside the arena. There are more PATIENTS in the background listening. The entire group composes a tableau. The bath, in which MARAT stands, is wheeled in through the door at the back right.

CHORUS in sections:

A drawn-out cat-call.

A long monotonous whistle.

A muffled trampling of feet.

MARAT is pushed in his bath to the centre of the

arena. He stands straight and looks towards the HERALD.]

HERALD: Marat is still in his bathtub confined
but politicians crowd into his mind
He speaks to them his last polemic fight
to say who should be tribune It is almost night
> [*He gives the orchestra a sign with his staff.*
> *A flourish. The people in the tableau spring to*
> *life, stamp their feet, whistle and shout.*]

KOKOL: Down with Marat
CUCURUCU: Don't let him speak
ROSSIGNOL: Listen to him he's got the right to speak
POLPOCH: Long live Marat
KOKOL: Long live Robespierre
CUCURUCU: Long live Danton
MARAT: [*addressing the audience. During his entire speech he*
never turns to those present on the stage. It is obvious
that his speech is imaginary.]
Fellow citizens
members of the National Assembly
our country is in danger
From every corner of Europe armies invade us
led by profiteers
who want to strangle us
and already quarrel over the spoils
And what are we doing
> [*apathetic noises*]
Our minister of war
whose integrity you never doubted
has sold the corn meant for our armies
for his own profit to foreign powers
and now it feeds the troops
who are invading us
> [*Cries and whistles.*]
KOKOL: Lies

CUCURUCU:	Throw him out
MARAT:	The chief of our army Dumouriez
ROSSIGNOL:	Bravo
POLPOCH:	Long live Dumouriez
MARAT:	against whom I've warned you continually
	and whom you recently hailed as a hero
	has gone over to the enemy
KOKOL:	Shame
ROSSIGNOL:	Bravo
CUCURUCU:	Liar
	[*shuffling of feet*]
MARAT:	Most of the generals
	who wear our uniform
	are sympathetic with the emigrés
	and when the emigrés return
	our generals will be out to welcome them
KOKOL:	Execute them
CUCURUCU:	Down with Marat
ROSSIGNOL:	Bravo
POLPOCH:	Long live Marat
MARAT:	Our trusted minister of finance
	the celebrated Monsieur Cambon
	is issuing fake banknotes thus increasing inflation
	and diverting a fortune into his own pocket
	[*whistles and stamping*]
ROSSIGNOL:	Long live free enterprise
MARAT:	And I am told
	that Perregeaux our most intelligent banker
	is in league with the English
	and in his armoured vaults
	is organising a centre of espionage against us
COULMIER:	[*jumping up to protest*]
	That's enough
	We're living in eighteen hundred and eight

	and the names which were dragged through the gutter then
	have been deservedly rehabilitated
	by the command of the Emperor
ROSSIGNOL:	Go on
KOKOL:	Shut up Marat
CUCURUCU:	Shut his mouth
POLPOCH:	Long live Marat
MARAT:	[*interrupting*]

The people can't pay the inflated price of bread
Our soldiers march in rags
The counter-revolution has started a new civil
   war
and what are we doing
The farms we confiscated from the churches
   have so far produced nothing
to feed the dispossessed
and years have passed since I proposed these
   farms
should be divided into allotments
and given farm implements and seed
And why have we seen no communal workshops
which were to be started in the old monasteries
   and country houses
Those who have jobs
must sweat for agents stockbrokers and specu-
   lators
[*wild cries*]
Fellow citizens
did we fight for the freedom of those
who now exploit us again

KOKOL:	Sit down
ROSSIGNOL:	Hear hear
CUCURUCU:	Sit down

POLPOCH: Hear hear
MARAT: Our country is in danger
We talk about France
but who is France for
We talk about freedom
but who's this freedom for
Members of the National Assembly
you will never shake off the past
you'll never understand
the great upheaval in which you find yourselves
[*whistles and cries of Boo*]
Why aren't there thousands of public seats
in this assembly
so anyone who wants
can hear what's being discussed
DUPERRET: What is he trying to do
He's trying to rouse the people again
Look who sits on the public benches
Knitting-women concierges and washerwomen
with no one to employ them any more
And who has he got on his side
Pickpockets layabouts parasites
who loiter in the boulevards
[*indignation among the onlookers*]
and hang around the cafes
CUCURUCU: Wish we could
DUPERRET: Released prisoners
escaped lunatics
[*tumult and whistling*]
Does he want to rule our country
with these
MARAT: You are liars
You hate the people
[*cries of indignation*]
ROSSIGNOL: Well done Marat

POLPOCH: That's true
MARAT: You'll never stop talking of the people
             as a rough and formless mass
             Why
             Because you live apart from them
             You let yourselves be dragged into the Revolu-
                 tion
             knowing nothing about its principles
             Has not our respected Danton himself an-
                 nounced
             that instead of banning riches
             we should try
             to make poverty respectable
             And Robespierre
             who turns white when the word force is used
             doesn't he sit at high-class tables
             making cultural conversation
             by candlelight
             [*tongue clicking*]
KOKOL: Shame
CUCURUCU: Down with Robespierre
POLPOCH: Long live Marat
ROSSIGNOL: Down with Danton
MARAT: And you still long to ape them
             those powdered chimpanzees
             Necker Lafayette Talleyrand
COULMIER: [*interrupting*]
             That's enough
             If you use any more of these passages
             we agreed to cut
             I will stop your play
MARAT: [*breaking in*]
             and all the rest of them
             What we need now is a true deputy of the
                 people

84

	one who's incorruptible
	one we can trust
	Things are breaking down things are chaotic
	that is good
	that's the first step
	Now we must take the next step
	and choose a man
	who will rule for you
ROSSIGNOL:	Marat for dictator
POLPOCH:	Marat in his bathtub
KOKOL:	Send him down the sewers
CUCURUCU:	Dictator of the rats
MARAT:	Dictator The word must be abolished
	I hate anything to do with masters and slaves
	I am talking about a leader
	who in this hour of crisis
	[*his words are drowned in the mighty tumult*]
DUPERRET:	He's trying to incite them
	to new murders
MARAT:	We do not murder
	we kill in self-defence
	We are fighting
	for our lives
DUPERRET:	Oh if only we could have constructive thought
	instead of agitation
	If only beauty and concord could once more replace
	hysteria and fanaticism
	[*The* FOUR SINGERS *throw themselves on* DUPERRET *and stop his mouth.*]
ROUX:	[*jumping up in the background*]
	Look what's happening
	Join together
	Cast down your enemies
	disarm them

For if they win
they will spare
not one of you
and all that you have won so far
will be lost
      [*Enthusiastic calls, whistles and trampling.*]

CALLS: [*in spoken chorus, simultaneously*]
Marat Marat Marat Marat
Boo
A laurel wreath for Marat
Down with Marat
A victory parade for Marat
Down with him
Long live the streets
Long live the lamp-posts
Long live the bakers' shops
Long live freedom
      [*Disorder and screams. The* PATIENTS *tumble
forward.* MARAT's *bath is pushed on to the
platform right.*]

KOKOL &   [*dancing*]
POLPOCH: Hit at the rich until they crash
Throw down their god and divide their cash

CUCURUCU &   [*dancing*]
ROSSIGNOL: We wouldn't mind a tasty meal
of paté de foie and filleted eel

CHORUS: Marat Marat Marat Marat Marat
      [SADE *raises his hands. They all freeze.
Roll of drums and beginning of music.*]

28. POOR MARAT IN YOUR BATHTUB SEAT

      [MARAT *sinks back into his bath. Exhausted,
he leans forward on the board.
The spectators' benches are pushed back, the*

FOUR
SINGERS:

SISTERS *and* NURSES *force back the* PATIENTS.
In front of the arena the FOUR SINGERS *dance
a slow Carmagnole.*]
[*accompanied, singing and dancing*]
Poor Marat in your bathtub seat
your life on this planet is near complete
Closer and closer to you death creeps
though there on her bench Charlotte Corday
    sleeps

Poor Marat if she slept too late
while dreaming of fairy-tale heads of state
maybe your sickness would disappear
Charlotte Corday would not find you here

Poor Marat stay wide awake
and be on your guard for the people's sake
Stare through the failing evening light
for this is the evening before the night

> [*Drums. In the background order has been
> restored after a fashion. The patients should be
> standing upright, their hands crossed above their
> heads.* SISTERS *are standing before them, folding
> their hands and praying. The murmur of prayers
> can be heard. The* FOUR SINGERS *dance on a
> while and then stretch themselves out on the arena
> before* MARAT's *bath.*]

MARAT:

[*with fear in his voice*]
What is that knocking Simonne
[*tyrannic again*]
Simonne
more cold water
> [SIMONNE *sits huddled up at the edge of the
> platform and doesn't react.*]
Simonne

87

	Where is Bas
SADE:	Give up Marat
	You said yourself
	nothing can be achieved by scribbling
	Long ago I abandoned my masterpiece
	a roll of paper thirty yards long
	which I filled completely with minute hand-writing
	in my dungeon years ago
	It vanished when the Bastille fell
	it vanished as everything written
	everything thought and planned
	will disappear

[MARAT *lies with his face on the board and covers his ears with his hands.*]

SADE:	[*continues*]
	Marat
	Look at me
	Marat can you call this living
	in your bath
	in your mortification

[*By order of the* SISTERS *the* PATIENTS *change their position and stretch up their hands.*]

MARAT:	[*raising himself up*]
	I had time for nothing but work
	Day and night were not enough for me
	When I investigated a wrong it grew branches
	and every branch grew twigs
	Wherever I turned
	I found corruption

[*A* PATIENT *falls over in the ranks. A* NURSE *carries him off.*]

When I wrote
I always wrote with action in mind
kept sight of the fact

that writing was just a preparation
When I wrote
I always wrote in a fever
hearing the roar of action
When I was preparing
my book on the chains of slavery
I sat for three months
twenty-one hours a day
collecting material dreaming of material
paper piling high parchment crackling
until I sank into the swamps of overwork
That manuscript was suppressed
They were always ready
to pick up my statements
to slander them maim them
After each pamphlet was published
I had to go into hiding
They came with cannons
A thousand men of the National Guard
surrounded my house
And even today
I still wait for the knocking at the door
wait
for the bayonet to point at my breast
Simonne
Simonne
Fetch Bas
so that I can dictate my call
my fourteenth of July call

SADE: Why all these calls to the nation
It's too late Marat
forget your call
it contains only lies
What do you still want from the revolution
Where is it going

Look at these lost revolutionaries

[*Pointing to the* FOUR SINGERS *who lie stretched out on the floor, scratching themselves, yawning and trying to get the last drop out of the empty bottle.*]

What will you order them to do
Where will you lead them

[*In the background the* PATIENTS, *on the* SISTERS' *command, must stand on one leg.*]

Once you attacked the authorities who turned
the law into instruments of oppression
But Marat how will you fare in the new re-
arranged France you yearn for
Do you want someone to rule you
to control the words you write
and tell you
what work you must do
and repeat to you the new laws
over and over
until you can recite them in your sleep

[*The* PATIENTS *in the background walk in a circle while the* SISTERS *pray. The* FOUR SINGERS *begin to hum unconcernedly, lying at first on the floor with legs waving in the air. Then* ROSSIGNOL *and* CUCURUCU *get up and dance to the hummed melody.*]

MARAT: [*falling across the board again*]
Why is everything so confused now
Everything I wrote or spoke
was considered and true
each argument was sound
And now
doubt
Why does everything sound false

THE FOUR
SINGERS:

[*singing and dancing*]
Poor old Marat you lie prostrate
While others are gambling with France's fate
Your words have turned into a flood
which covers all France with her people's
blood
[*Music ends. The* FOUR SINGERS *dance back to
the centre of the stage. The* PATIENTS *are led to
their platform. The* SISTERS *try to wake*
CORDAY. *Loud knocking three times.*]

29. PREPARATIONS FOR THE THIRD VISIT

HERALD:

Corday
wake up
[*Pause. The name* CORDAY *is whispered in the
background. The whispering swells up and
spreads over the whole stage. The* SISTERS *shake*
CORDAY, DUPERRET *calls her name.*
SIMONNE *stands awkwardly by the bath and
gazes across at* CORDAY.]

CHORUS:

Corday
Corday
Corday

HERALD:

[*signals to the orchestra with his staff*]
Corday you have an appointment to keep
and there is no more time for sleep
Charlotte Corday awake and stand
Take the dagger in your hand
[*Pause. The* SISTERS *raise* CORDAY *to her feet.*
CORDAY *stands with lowered head and wobbly
legs. The* SISTERS *support her and lead her
slowly forward. Her legs drag along the floor.*
DUPERRET *walks behind her with his hands
around her hips.*]

HERALD: Come on Charlotte do your deed
soon you'll get all the sleep you need
[CORDAY *is pushed into the arena. The two*
SISTERS *stand at her side holding her firmly.*
DUPERRET, *standing behind her, supports her*
back. Music ends.]

CORDAY: [*her eyes still closed, speaking softly, nervously*]
Now I know what it is like
when the head is cut off the body
Oh this moment
hands tied behind the back
feet bound together
neck bared
hair cut off
knees on the boards
the head already laid
in the metal slot
looking down into the dripping basket
The sound of the blade rising
and from its slanting edge
the blood still drops
and then the downward slide
to split us in two
[*pause*]
They say
that the head
held high in the executioner's hand
still lives
that the eyes still see
that the tongue still writhes
and down below the arms and legs still shudder

DUPERRET: [*accompanied by lute. He is still holding his hand on*
her hip.]
Charlotte awaken from your nightmare
Wake up Charlotte and look at the trees

look at the rose-coloured evening sky
in which your lovely bosom heaves
Forget your worries abandon each care
and breathe in the warmth of the summer-time air
[*Pause. He lifts his hand and strokes her on the*
bosom. He notices the dagger under the cloth.]
What are you hiding
A dagger
throw it away
[*the music ends*]

CORDAY: [*pushes his hand away*]
We should all carry weapons nowadays
in self-defence

DUPERRET: [*beseechingly*]
No one will attack you Charlotte
Charlotte throw the dagger away
go away
go back to Caen

CORDAY: [*drawing herself up and pushing the* SISTERS' *hands*
away]
In my room in Caen
on the table under the open window
lies open The Book of Judith
Dressed in her legendary beauty
she entered the tent of the enemy
and with a single blow
slew him

DUPERRET: Charlotte
what are you planning

CORDAY: [*forlorn again*]
Look at this city
Its prisons are crowded
with our friends
I was among them just now
in my sleep

	They all stand huddled together there
	and hear through the windows
	the guards talking about executions
	Now they talk of people as gardeners talk of
	leaves for burning
	Their names are crossed off the top of a list
	and as the list grows shorter
	more names are added at the bottom
	I stood with them
	and we waited
	for our own names to be called
DUPERRET:	Charlotte
	let us leave together
	this very evening
CORDAY:	[*as if she has not heard him*]
	What kind of town is this
	What sort of streets are these
	Who invented this
	who profits by it
	I saw peddlers
	at every corner
	they're selling little guillotines
	with tiny sharp blades
	and dolls filled with red liquid
	which spurts from the neck
	when the sentence is carried out
	What kind of children are these
	who can play
	with this toy so efficiently
	and who is judging
	who is judging

> [PATIENTS *move to a group at centre.* CORDAY
> *raises her hand to knock.*]

94

30. CORDAY'S THIRD AND LAST VISIT

[*The* HERALD *knocks three times on the floor with his staff while* CORDAY *carries out the knocking movement with her hand.*
MARAT *starts up and looks in* CORDAY'S *direction.*
SIMONNE *places herself protectively in front of the bath.*]

DUPERRET: What do you want at this door
Do you know who lives here

CORDAY: The man
for whose sake I have come here

DUPERRET: What do you want from him
Turn back Charlotte
[*goes on his knees before her*]

CORDAY: I have a task
which I must carry out
Go
[*pushes him with her foot*]
leave me alone
[DUPERRET *embraces her legs. She kicks out at him several times.* DUPERRET *moves back on his knees.*]

HERALD: Now for the third time you observe
the girl whose job it is to serve
[*points to* CORDAY]
as Charlotte Corday stands once more
waiting outside Marat's door
Duperret you see before her languish
[*points to* DUPERRET]
prostrated by their parting's anguish
[*raising a forefinger*]
For what has happened cannot be undone

95

although that might be wished by everyone
[*pointing to* CORDAY]
We tried restraining her with peaceful sleep
and with the claims of a passion still more deep
Simonne as well as best she could she tried
[*pointing to* SIMONNE]
but this girl here
[*points to* CORDAY]
would not be turned aside
That man is now forgotten and we can
[*points to* DUPERRET *who moves backwards on his knees from the dais*]
do nothing more Corday is focussed on this man
[*points to* MARAT]

MARAT: No
[*raising himself high*]
I am right
and I will say it once more
Simonne
where is Bas
It is urgent
my call

       [SIMONNE *moves aside, stops still and stares
       bewitched at* CORDAY.]

SADE: [*approaches the bath*]
Marat
what are all your pamphlets and speeches
compared with her
she stands there and will come to you
to kiss you and embrace you
Marat
an untouched virgin stands before you and
   offers herself to you
See how she smiles

       [CORDAY *stands erect and smiling, throwing*

her hair aside. She has her hand on the neckcloth
in the place where the dagger is hidden.]
how her teeth shine
how she shakes her auburn hair aside
Marat
forget the rest
there's nothing else
beyond the body
Look
she stands there
her breast naked under the thin cloth
and perhaps she carries a knife
to intensify the love-play
    [CORDAY *moves a step closer to the bath,*
    swaying lightly. SIMONNE *stands frozen,*
    mechanically wringing the cloth in her hands.]

MARAT: Simonne Simonne
who was knocking at the door
SADE: A maiden
from the rural desert of a convent
Imagine
those pure girls lying on hard floors
in rough shifts
and the heated air from the fields
forcing its way to them through the barred
    windows
Imagine
them lying there
with moist thighs and breasts
dreaming of those
who control life in the outside world
    [*The* FOUR SINGERS *come forward and begin*
    a copulation mime.
    ROSSIGNOL *mounts the strongest of her*
    companions and performs acrobatics with them.]

SADE: [*to musical accompaniment*]
And then she was tired of her isolation
and stirred up by the new age
and gathered up in the great tide
and wanted to be part of the Revolution
And what's the point of a revolution
without general copulation

CHORUS: And what's the point of a revolution
without general
copulation copulation copulation
[*continues as a round. Mime ends.*]

SADE: Marat
as I sat there in the Bastille
for thirteen long years
I learned
that this is a world of bodies
each body pulsing with a terrible power
each body alone and racked with its own unrest
In that loneliness
marooned in a stone sea
I heard lips whispering continually
and felt all the time
in the palms of my hands and in my skin
touching and stroking
Shut behind thirteen bolted doors
my feet fettered
I dreamed only
of the orifices of the body
put there
so one may hook and twine oneself in them
[*A* PATIENT *comes forward on tip-toe and stops
behind the arena, listening tensely. Other*
PATIENTS *follow.*]
Continually I dreamed of this confrontation
and it was a dream of the most savage jealous

98

and cruellest imagining
Marat
these cells of the inner self
are worse than the deepest stone dungeon
and as long as they are locked
all your revolution remains
only a prison mutiny
to be put down
by corrupted fellow-prisoners

CHORUS: [*repeating with musical accompaniment*]
And what's the point of a revolution
without general copulation
    [*Music ends.*]

CORDAY: [*to* SIMONNE. *Lute accompaniment.*]
Have you given my letter to Marat
Let me in it is vital
I must tell him what's happening in Caen
where they are gathering to destroy him

MARAT: Who's at the door

SIMONNE: The girl from Caen

MARAT: Let her come in

    [SIMONNE *stands aside, shaking her head
vigorously. She squats down at the edge of the
dais behind the bath and hides her head in her
hands.* CORDAY *moves towards the bath,
swaying and smiling. Her hand still rests on her
neckcloth.* SADE *leaves the arena and goes to his
dais, where he remains, standing, watching
tensely.*]

CORDAY: [*softly*]
Marat
I will tell you the names of my heroes
but I am not betraying them
for I am speaking to a dead man

MARAT: [*raising himself up*]

99

Speak more clearly
I can't understand you
Come closer

CORDAY: [*coming closer to the bath with a fixed smile, her body slowly swaying. She pushes a hand under her neck-cloth.*]
I name you names
Marat
the names of those
who have gathered at Caen
[*falling into a sing-song*]
I name Barbaroux
and Buzot
and Pétion
and Louvet
[*as she speaks the names her face is distorted increasingly by an expression of hate and lust*]
and Brissot
and Vergniaud
and Guadet
and Gensonné

MARAT: Who are you
Come closer
[MARAT *raises himself up high. The cloth falls from his shoulders.* CORDAY *moves closer to him, swaying. Her left hand is stretched out as if to caress. In the right hand she holds the dagger under the neckcloth.*]

CORDAY: [*humming words which sound like caresses*]
I am coming Marat
You cannot see me Marat
because you are dead

MARAT: [*crying out, raising himself up high, half-naked*]
Bas
Take this down

Saturday the thirteenth of July seventeen
hundred and ninety three
A call to the people of France

> [CORDAY *stands immediately before* MARAT.
> *She moves her left hand close to his skin over his
> chest, his shoulders, his neck.* MARAT *sits arched
> over the back of the bath, a pen still in his hand.*
> CORDAY *pulls the dagger from her neckcloth.
> She holds it with both hands and raises her arms
> high to strike.*
> *The* HERALD *blows shrilly on his whistle.
> All players remain unmoving in their positions.*
> CORDAY *sinks back into herself.* MARAT *sits
> quietly, leaning forward.*]

31. INTERRUPTUS

HERALD: Now it's a part of Sade's dramatic plan
            to interrupt the climax so this man
            Marat can hear and gasp with his last breath
            at how the world will go after his death
            With a musical history we'll bring him up to
                date
            From seventeen-ninety-three to eighteen-eight

> [*Music starts with very quick military march.
> The* FOUR SINGERS *sing and perform gro-
> tesquely in time to the music. The* HERALD
> *displays banners showing the date of the events
> as they are described.*]

FOUR   Now your enemies fall*
SINGERS: We're beheading them all [*1793*]
            Duperret
            and Corday
            executed in the same old way

* A literal verse translation of this section appears on page 108

Robespierre has to get on [*1794*]
he gets rid of Danton
That was spring
comes July
and old Robespierre has to die
Three rebellions a year [*1795*]
but we're still of good cheer
Malcontents
all have been
taught their lesson by the guillotine
There's a shortage of wheat [*1796*]
We're too happy to eat
Austria
cracks and then
she surrenders to our men

Fifteen glorious years
Fifteen glorious years
Years of peace
years of war
each year greater
than the year before
Marat
we're marching on

What brave soldiers we've got [*1797*]
Now the traitors are shot
Generals
boldly take
power in Paris
for the people's sake
Egypt's beaten down flat [*1798*]
Bonaparte did that
Cheer him as
they retreat
even though we lose our fleet

Bonaparte comes back [*1799*]
gives our rulers the sack
He's the man [*1800*]
brave and true
Bonaparte would die for you
Europe's free of her chains [*1801*]
Only England remains
but we want [*1802*]
wars to cease
so there's fourteen months of peace

[PATIENTS *join in, marching on the spot*]
Fifteen glorious years
Fifteen glorious years
Years of peace
years of war
each year greater
than the year before
Marat
we're marching on

England must be insane [*1803*]
wants to fight us again
so we march
off to war
Bonaparte is our Emperor [*1804*]
Nelson bothers our fleet
but he's shot off his feet
We're on top
yes we are
and we spit on Trafalgar
Now the Prussians retreat [*1806*]
Russia faces defeat [*1807*]
All the world
bends its knee
to Napoleon

and his family
Fight on land and on sea [*1808*]
All men want to be free
If they don't
never mind
we'll abolish all mankind

Fifteen glorious years
Fifteen glorious years
Years of peace
years of war
each year greater
than the one before
Marat
we're marching on
behind Napoleon

32. THE MURDER

[*The* HERALD *makes a sign with his staff.*]

HERALD: The murder

[CORDAY, *suddenly wide awake, raises her arms up and brings the dagger violently down in* MARAT'S *breast.*

PATIENTS *let out one single scream.*

SADE *stands leaning forward, triumphant, shaken by silent laughter.*

All stand around the bath in a tableau composed as follows: MARAT *hangs, as in David's famous picture, with his right arm over the edge of the bath. In his right hand he holds a pen, in his left his papers.* CORDAY *is still clasping the dagger. The* FOUR SINGERS *have seized her from behind and forced back her arms until her neckcloth bursts open showing her breast.* SIMONNE *bends over the bath with an expression*

of horror. DUPERRET *is on his knees.* ROUX
stands bolt upright on a bench behind the bath.]

33. EPILOGUE

[*The* ORCHESTRA *starts to play soft ceremonious music. The* SISTERS *come forward and
take charge of* CORDAY, *who now sinks back
into herself. They replace the neckcloth and lead
her towards* SADE.
CORDAY *gives the dagger to* SADE.
SISTERS *hold a large white sheet in front of the
bath. Behind it* MARAT *gets out of the bath.
The* HERALD *comes forward and raises his
staff.
The music ends.*

HERALD: Enlightened ladies pious gentlemen
let's close the history book and then
return to eighteen-eight the present day
of which though not unclouded we may say
it promises that mankind soon will cease
to fear the storms of war the squalls of peace
Before you go out into the street
let us now just briefly repeat
what we have all been trying to say
in the words and music of our play
So we will now call back to life
the man who just died by the knife

      [*The sheet is lowered.* MARAT *comes forward.*]

MARAT: We have only one single life on earth
so what I'll say has little worth
In my only life I had to make
my choice about which path to take
The world I saw around me then
was ruled by one small group of men
They were the few who held the money-bags

105

while all the others went about in rags
So I decided that my only course
must be to smash their laws by force
pull down the men who sat there tight
pretending that they ruled by right
and saying that equality was an illusion
the fight for profit must go on
As a corpse I'm not much use to you
but all the things I taught were true
and others now will carry on
the fight that I Marat begun
until one day the hour will strike
when men will share and share alike

ROUX: [*advancing quickly*]
If I were still alive I'd say beware
of this young woman here
[*pointing to* CORDAY]
For time and again we are forced to pay
for those who choose the idealist's way
who talk of purity and spiritual aims
while playing the oppressors' games
More dangerous than those with all their
    wealth
is this girl here for she works by stealth
In some we can easily recognise our foe
but what she is after we can never know
    [*At a sign from* COULMIER, SISTERS *and*
    NURSES *run towards* ROUX *and drag him off.*]

HERALD: [*turning to* SADE]
Now tell us please Monsieur de Sade
what you have achieved with this charade
Has this drama in our bath hall
elucidated anything at all

SADE: Our play's chief aim has been to take to bits
great propositions and their opposites

see how they work then let them fight it out
The point   Some light on our eternal doubt
I have twisted and turned them every way
and find no ending to our play
Marat and I both advocated force
but in debate each took a different course
Each wanted changes but his views and mine
on using power never can combine
On the one side he who thinks our lives
can be improved with axes and knives
Or the who'd submerge in his imagination
seeking a personal annihilation
So for me the last word can never be spoken
I am left with a question that is always open

COULMIER: But today we live in far different times
We have no oppressors no violent crimes
We are well on the way to achieving our goal
There's bread in plenty and there's also coal
And although we're at war anyone can see
it can only end in victory

> [*The* ORCHESTRA *beings to play the final
> march. The* PATIENTS *start to mark time.*]

FOUR
SINGERS: And if most have a little and few have a lot
you can see how much nearer our goal we have
    got
We can say what we like without favour or fear
and what we can't say we can breathe in your
    ear

ALL: [*marking time as the music grows louder*]
And though we're locked up we're no longer
    enslaved
and the honour of France is eternally saved
The useless debate the political brawl
are over   There's one man to speak for us all
For he helps us in sickness and destitution

He's the leader who ended the Revolution
and everyone knows why we're cheering for
Napoleon our mighty Emperor

> [*A banner bearing an idealised portrait of
> Napoleon is let down. The music increases in
> volume. The column of* PATIENTS *begins to
> march forward.* SISTERS *and* NURSES *try to
> restrain it. Several times the column takes four
> paces forward and three paces back. The music
> and marching rhythm grow in power.*
> COULMIER *moves anxiously to the side, gesticu-
> lating.*]

ALL: Led by him our soldiers go
over deserts and through the snow
A victory here and a victory there
Invincible glorious always victorious
for the good of all people everywhere

> [*The column advances still further, stamping
> some paces forward and some back.*]

COULMIER: [*shouting through the tumult*]
Long live the Emperor and the nation
Long live our clinic
Charenton

ALL: [*in confused but rhythmic shouts in time to the
marching*]
Charenton Charenton
Napoleon Napoleon
Nation Nation
Revolution Revolution
Copulation Copulation

ROUX: [*shouting through the noise*]
When will you learn to see

> [*Music, shouting and stamping increase to a
> hurricane.* COULMIER *rushes to his tribunal and
> sounds an alarm bell. The* NURSES *go among*

　　　　　　　　　the patients wielding their batons. ROUX
　　　　　　　　　hurries forward.]

ROUX:　　　　　[*to the patients and the audience*]
　　　　　　　　　When will you learn to see
　　　　　　　　　When will you ever understand

　　　　　　　　　[ROUX *throws himself backwards against the
　　　　　　　　　marchers, trying to force them back. But he is
　　　　　　　　　drawn in and vanishes from sight in the still
　　　　　　　　　advancing ranks. The* PATIENTS *are fully at the
　　　　　　　　　mercy of their mad marchlike dance. Many of
　　　　　　　　　them hop and spin in ecstasy.*

　　　　　　　　　COULMIER *incites the* NURSES *to extreme
　　　　　　　　　violence.* PATIENTS *are struck down.*

　　　　　　　　　The HERALD *is now in front of the orchestra,
　　　　　　　　　leaping about in time to the music.*

　　　　　　　　　SADE *stands upright on his chair, laughing
　　　　　　　　　triumphantly.*

　　　　　　　　　In desperation COULMIER *gives the signal to
　　　　　　　　　close the curtain.*]

　　　　　　　　　　　　CURTAIN

In the Vendée the battle rages
with deeds both cruel and courageous
between our men and the king's supporters
and we drive them from their quarters
With flying banners we march along
an avenging army with fire and song
called Regiment Marat in your renown
and with it we mow our enemies down
Marat the things you bade us do
we now with all our strength put through
Our foes lie beaten in the sand
or take their lives with their own hand
And with cannon and horse we march along
and storm the counter-revolutionary throng
in Lyon where for example's sake
we send three thousand to the stake
And now through Nantes our army passes
where we drown citizens in masses
and every house where a rebel is found
we raze relentlessly to the ground
And at last with flying banners we come
to the traitor city of Toulon
and with us is one whose star is ascending
who can lead us on to victories unending
You see Marat how we advance

* page 101

and now we begin to thin our own ranks
Just as you told us so must above all
the weak and incapable go to the wall
Robespierre puts Danton to the axe
and sends in his wake with all despatch
many of our old confederates
on whom in our ignorance we'd based our hopes
Marat we cannot believe it's true
what our new bosses start to do
Beside the nobles we see in the carts
Jacobins who were once dear to our hearts
and the axe treats them all regardless of name
and when they are corpses they look all the same
Marat we can only stand and gape
at the curious moods of fate
Now we see Robespierre bound and trussed
and already his head has rolled in the dust
Marat how does this all fit together
that the one lot always condemns the other
Tell us Marat must it be so
that someone above for the sake of show
must always direct and always lead
and in the doing it forfeit his head
Marat to comfort you we can say
whom we now have with us today
Napoleon Bonaparte now stands there
like you comes from Corsica or Sardinia
and he has promised us peace eternal
and gives us work in the arsenal
and in honour of the revolution
he calls himself emperor Napoleon
It is we can tell you a feast for the eye
and with rumbling bellies we watch it go by
We just stand and stare
and the holy men bless us in prayer

Even before his confinement in the stronghold of Vincennes and the Paris Bastille Sade had produced plays in his residence La Coste. During the thirteen years of his imprisonment, between the ages of 33 and 46, he wrote seventeen plays in addition to his large prose works. In later years he brought out a further dozen tragedies, comedies, operas, pantomimes and one-acters in verse. Out of all these pieces only one, *Oxstiern ou les malheurs du libertinage*, was performed in a public theatre during his years of liberty 1790–1801—and taken off at once after a scandal.

From 1801 until his death in 1814 Sade was interned in the asylum of Charenton, where over a period of years he had the chance of producing plays among the patients and appearing as an actor himself. Charenton (to follow J. L. Casper's description in his *Charakteristik der französischen Medizin*, published in 1822 in Leipzig) was an institution which catered for all whose behaviour had made them socially impossible, whether they were lunatics or not. Here were locked up 'perpetrators of crimes whose handling in open court would not be in the public interest, as well as others who had been arrested for serious political misdemeanours or who had allowed themselves to be used as the evil tools of high intrigues'.

In exclusive Paris circles it was considered a rare pleasure to attend Sade's theatrical performances in the 'hiding-place for the moral rejects of civilised society'. It is of course probable that these amateur performances consisted in the main of declamatory pieces in the prevailing style: the bulk of Sade's dramatic work does not reach up to the boldness and consistency of his prose. But in his *Dialogue entre un prêtre et un moribund* and above all in *La philosophie dans le boudoir* there are analytical and philosophical conversations, carried out against a background of bodily excess, which clearly show his dramatic perception. His visual mode of thought is also seen again and again in the exceptionally realistic descriptive passages of the novels.

Sade's encounter with Marat, which is the subject of this play, is entirely imaginary, based only on the single fact that it was Sade who spoke the memorial address at Marat's funeral. Even in this speech his real attitude towards Marat is questionable, since he made the speech primarily to save his own skin; at that time his position was in danger, his name on the list of those marked out for the guillotine.

What interests me in bringing together Sade and Marat is the conflict between an individualism carried to extreme lengths and the idea of a political and social upheaval. Even Sade knew the Revolution to be necessary: his works are one single attack on a corrupt ruling class. He flinched however from the violent methods of the progressives and, like the modern advocate of a third approach, fell between two stools. He did indeed, on his release from prison in 1790, place himself at the service of the National Assembly and became an official in the *Section des Piques*, where he was put in charge of hospitals. He was even made a judge. But the long years of imprisonment had left their mark on him: he remained an outsider and found contact with his fellow men difficult.

His claim that he had suffered at the hands of the old regime cannot be taken as evidence of heroism, since his imprisonment was due to charges of sexual extravagance and not to political acts. These excesses, in monstrous written form, were once again to cause his downfall under the new regime.

Sade's own picture of himself as a rebel can be seen in a letter written from prison to his wife in 1783, in which he says:

'You say that one cannot approve my mode of thought. What does that signify? Anyone who imagines he can prescribe a mode of thought to another must be quite out of his senses. My mode of thought is the result of my own reflections, it is a part of my life, of my own nature. It is not in my power to alter it, and if it were in my power I should not do it. This mode of thought which you condemn is the only comfort of my life: it relieves all my sufferings in prison, it provides all my pleasure in this world; it means more to me than my own life. It is not my mode of thought that has caused my misfortunes, but the mode of thought of others.'

It is difficult to imagine Sade in the role of a worker for the common good. He felt himself obliged to adopt a double-faced attitude. On the one hand he approved Marat's radical arguments, on the other he saw the dangers of totalitarianism. His views on the fair division of worldly goods did not go to the length that he could contemplate giving up his own house and property, and he did not submit tamely when forced to give up La Coste after it had been plundered and burnt.

Sade's plays represent his last attempt to communicate with his fellow beings, but with advancing age he relapsed entirely into solitariness. A doctor at Charenton wrote, 'I frequently encountered him as he walked alone, with heavy dragging steps, very negligently dressed, through the corridors near his home. I never saw him speak with anybody. I would greet him as I passed by and he would return my greeting with a cold politeness that precluded any thought of conversation.'

If the idea of bringing Sade into contact with Marat in his final hour is my own invention, the picture of Marat at this time accords with fact. The psychosomatic skin disease from which he suffered in the last years of his life—a legacy of privation in the cellars in which he hid—forced him to spend many hours in the bath in order to soothe his itching. And here he was on Saturday, 13 July 1793, when Charlotte Corday came three times to his door before she gained entry and stabbed him.

Marat's words in the play correspond in content and often almost exactly in expression with the writings he left behind. What is said about the various phases of his life is also authentic. He left home at the age of sixteen, studied medicine, lived for some years in England, was renowned as a physician, misunderstood as a scientist, won social honours. Subsequently, however, after subjecting society to the shafts of his criticism, he placed himself entirely in the service of the Revolution and, on account of his violent and uncompromising character, was made the scapegoat for many acts of cruelty.

It was not until the beginning of the present century that writers like Rosbroy, Bax and Gottschalk began to revise the usual one-sided view of Marat and to draw attention to the acuteness of his political and scientific arguments. Scarcely any other personality of the French Revolution has been depicted in so revolting and bloodthirsty a light by the bourgeois historians of the nineteenth century as Marat. This is not really surprising, since his ideas lead in a direct line to Marxism, though they also come perilously near to the idea of dictatorship, even when he himself protested, 'Dictator: the word must be abolished. I hate anything to do with masters and slaves.'

From our vantage point today we must bear in mind that Marat was one of those who were in the process of building the socialist image, and that much in his ideas of change by forceful means was still undigested or overreached itself. Beside him in the play I have placed the former priest Jacques Roux, who surpassed Marat in his rabble-rousing and passionate pacifism. I have ignored the fact that Marat in the last days of his life turned away from Roux and, perhaps in an attack of persecution mania, disowned him. Roux, one of the most fascinating personalities of the Revolution, is here given the function of a champion and perfectionist, an *alter ego* against whom Marat's ideas can be measured.

I have also taken liberties in the portrayal of Duperret, the Girondist deputy. Here he is shown as the conservative patriot, one of many thousands of similar sort. He is also pressed into service as Charlotte Corday's lover, a role held in reality by a M. Tournelis, who left Caen to join the royalist refugees in Koblenz. In leaving him out of account I have acted entirely in the spirit of the Revolution itself, in the confusion of which no one was very exact in the matter of accusations and recriminations: poor Duperret himself, for instance, to whom Charlotte Corday has been recommended by the rebel group in Caen, had to pay for their brief encounter with his head.

Charlotte Corday had in fact let nobody into her secret. Schooled by convent life in the art of ecstatic withdrawal, she went her way alone and, with thoughts of Joan of Arc and the biblical Judith in mind, made a saint out of herself.

PETER WEISS

MUSIC COMPOSED SPECIALLY FOR
THE FIRST BRITISH PRODUCTION OF
THE PLAY AT THE ALDWYCH
THEATRE, LONDON

by

R. C. PEASLEE

HOMAGE TO MARAT

LIVELY ♩ = 120 - 128

Gm   F MAJ.

FOUR YEARS AF-TER THE RE -VOL-U-TION AND THE OLD KING'S EX-E-CU-TION

Gm   F MAJ.

FOUR YEARS AF-TER RE -MEM-BER HOW THOSE COURT-I-ERS TOOK THEIR FI-NAL BOW

Gm   CHORUS   Cm   Bb MAJ.

STRING UP EV'-RY— A-RIS -TO -CRAT

Cm

OUT WITH THE PRIESTS LET THEM LIVE ON THEIR FAT

MARAT WE'RE POOR

BROAD ♩ = 84 -88

D MAJ.   Am

MA - RAT WE'RE POOR — AND THE POOR STAY POOR — MA-RAT DON'T

D MAJ.   Am   C MAJ.   D MAJ. Bm

MAKE — US WAIT AN-Y — MORE GIVE US OUR RIGHTS AND WE DON'T CARE

E MAJ.   Am   (SHOUTED)

HOW — WE WANT — OUR RE-VOL-U-TION NOW

CORDAY WALTZ

MODERATELY ♩ = 140
FAST

ONCE BOTH — OF US SAW THE WORLD — MUST GO — AND
CHANGE AS WE READ — IN GREAT — ROUS-SEAU BUT CHANGE-MEANT
ONE THING TO YOU — I SEE — AND SOME-THING QUITE DIF-F'RENT TO
ME THE VER-Y SAME WORDS— WE BOTH — HAVE
SAID — TO GIVE OUR I — DEALS — WINGS TO SPREAD — BUT
MY WAY WAS TRUE — WHILE FOR YOU — THE HIGH-WAY LEAD
O — VER MOUN -TAINS OF DEAD —

SONG AND MIME OF CORDAY'S ARRIVAL IN PARIS
(CHARLOTTE CORDAY)

CHAR-LOTTE COR-DAY CAME TO OUR TOWN HEARD THE PEOP-LE TALK-ING

SAW THE BAN-NERS WAVE WEAR-I-NESS HAD AL-MOST DRAGGED HER DOWN —

WEAR-I-NESS HAD DRAGGED HER DOWN —

THE TUMBREL SONG

DON'T SOIL YOUR PRET-TY LIT-TLE SHOES — THE GUT-TER'S DEEP AND

RED — CLIMB UP CLIMB UP AND TAKE A RIDE WITH ME — THE TUM-BREL DRIV-ER

SAID — BUT SHE NEV-ER SAID A WORD — NEV-ER TURNED HER

HEAD —

THE PEOPLE'S REACTION

WHY HAVE THEY GOT THE CASH   WHY HAVE THEY GOT THE POW-ER   WHY-WHY-WHY-WHY

WHY —— HAVE THEY GOT THE FRIENDS AT THE TOP ——   WHY HAVE THEY GOT THE

JOBS AT THE TOP ——   WE'VE GOT NOTH-ING —   AL-WAYS HAD NOTH-ING

NOTH-ING BUT HOLES   AND   MIL-LIONS OF THEM   LIV-ING IN HOLES

DY-ING IN HOLES —   HOLES IN OUR BEL-LIES AND   HOLES IN OUR CLOTHES

MA-RAT WE'RE   POOR ——   ETC.

THOSE FAT MONKEYS

THOSE FAT MON-KEYS ——   COV-ERED IN BANK-NOTES   HAVE CHAM-PAGNE AND

BRAN-DY ON TAP —   THEY'RE UP   TO THEIR   EYE-BALLS IN FRANC-NOTES

(THOSE FAT MONKEYS)

WE'RE - UP TO OUR NOS-ES IN CRAP

POOR OLD MARAT

Allegretto
♩ = 132

POOR OLD MA-RAT THEY HUNT YOU DOWN THE BLOOD-HOUNDS ARE SNIF-FING ALL

OV-ER THE TOWN — JUST YES-TER-DAY — YOUR PRINT-ING PRESS WAS

SMASHED NOW THEY'RE ASK-ING YOUR HOME ——— AD-DRESS —

Chorus

POOR - OLD MA-RAT THEY HUNT YOU DOWN — THE

BLOOD-HOUNDS ARE SNIF — FING ALL OV ——— ER THE TOWN ———

POOR OLD MA-RAT WE TRUST IN YOU ——

122

FIFTEEN GLORIOUS YEARS

FIF-TEEN GLOR-I-OUS YEARS FIF-TEEN GLOR-I-OUS YEARS YEARS OF PEACE YEARS OF WAR

EACH YEAR GREAT-ER THAN THE YEAR BE-FORE FIF-TEEN GLOR-I-OUS GLOR-I-OUS GLOR-I-OUS

YEARS —— MA-RAT —— WE'RE MARCH-ING ON —— BE-HIND —— NA-PO-LE-

ON —— MA-RAT — MA-RAT —— WE'RE MARCH-ING

ON —— BE-HIND —— NA-PO-LE-ON ——

FINALE

AND IF MOST HAVE A LIT-TLE AND FEW HAVE A LOT YOU CAN

SEE HOW MUCH NEAR-ER OUR GOAL WE HAVE GOT WE CAN SAY WHAT WE LIKE WITH-OUT

FA-VOR OR FEAR AND WHAT WE CAN'T SAY WE CAN BREATHE IN YOUR EAR —